CW01187123

Managing in a Political World

Also by Steve Leach

ABOLITION OR REFORM: The GLC and Metropolitan County Councils (*with Norman Flynn and Carol Vielba*)

BOTCHED BUSINESS: The Damaging Process of Local Government Reorganisation 2006–2008 (*with Michael Chisholm*)

ENABLING OR DISABLING LOCAL GOVERNMENT (with Howard Davis)

LOCAL POLITICAL LEADERSHIP (*with David Wilson*)

STRATEGIC PLANNING AND MANAGEMENT IN LOCAL GOVERNMENT (*with Chris Collinge*)

THE CHANGING ORGANISATION AND MANAGEMENT OF LOCAL GOVERNMENT (*with John Stewart and Kieran Walsh*)

THE CHANGING POLITICS OF LOCAL GOVERNMENT (*with John Gyford and Chris Game*)

THE CHANGING POLITICS OF LOCAL GOVERNMENT IN BRITAIN

Managing in a Political World

The Life Cycle of Local Authority Chief Executives

Steve Leach

palgrave
macmillan

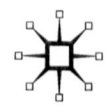

© Steve Leach 2010

All rights reserved. No reproduction, copy or transmission of this
publication may be made without written permission.

No portion of this publication may be reproduced, copied or transmitted
save with written permission or in accordance with the provisions of the
Copyright, Designs and Patents Act 1988, or under the terms of any licence
permitting limited copying issued by the Copyright Licensing Agency,
Saffron House, 6-10 Kirby Street, London EC1N 8TS.

Any person who does any unauthorized act in relation to this publication
may be liable to criminal prosecution and civil claims for damages.

The author has asserted his right to be identified
as the author of this work in accordance with the Copyright,
Designs and Patents Act 1988.

First published 2010 by
PALGRAVE MACMILLAN

Palgrave Macmillan in the UK is an imprint of Macmillan Publishers Limited,
registered in England, company number 785998, of Houndmills, Basingstoke,
Hampshire RG21 6XS.

Palgrave Macmillan in the US is a division of St Martin's Press LLC,
175 Fifth Avenue, New York, NY 10010.

Palgrave Macmillan is the global academic imprint of the above companies
and has companies and representatives throughout the world.

Palgrave® and Macmillan® are registered trademarks in the United States,
the United Kingdom, Europe and other countries.

ISBN: 978–0–230–24562–4 hardback

This book is printed on paper suitable for recycling and made from fully
managed and sustained forest sources. Logging, pulping and manufacturing
processes are expected to conform to the environmental regulations of the
country of origin.

A catalogue record for this book is available from the British Library.

Library of Congress Cataloging-in-Publication Data
Leach, Steve, 1942–
   Managing in a political world : the life cycle of local authority
chief executives / by Steve Leach.
     p.   cm.
   Includes bibliographical references.
   ISBN 978–0–230–24562–4
   1. Local government—Great Britain. 2. Government executives—
Great Britain. 3. Chief executive officers—Great Britain. I. Title.
   JS3158.L43 2010
   352.23′2140941—dc22
                                                                   2010027531

10 9 8 7 6 5 4 3 2 1
19 18 17 16 15 14 13 12 11 10

Printed and bound in Great Britain by
CPI Antony Rowe, Chippenham and Eastbourne

Contents

List of Tables vi

Preface vii

1 Introduction: Understanding the Challenges Facing Chief Executives 1
2 Taking the Job and Getting Started 26
3 The Chief Executive as 'Head of Paid Service' 38
4 Managing the Relationship with the Leader 48
5 Dealing with Political Change 62
6 The Chief Executive as a Political Animal 71
7 The Essence of a Good Relationship 83
8 Testing the Relationship 97
9 Moving On: By Choice or Otherwise 109
10 The Impact of Inspection and the Performance Culture 130
11 The Impact of the Move to Executive Government 150
12 Where Next for Chief Executives 164

Postscript 194

Notes 202
Bibliography 205
Index 207

List of Tables

8.1	Categories of critical incidents	98
12.1	Causes of breakdown in leader/chief executive relationships	169
12.2	Three Models of Officer Structure: Key Features	181

Preface

This book is the outcome of a long-term interest in the relationships between leading members and officers (and in particular between political leaders and chief executives) in British local authorities. As a (very) junior planning officer in Manchester City Council in the late 1960s, I noted with interest the way in which the City Planning Officer reacted angrily to the characterisation of planning by the leaders of the new Conservative administration as 'nugatory' (without myself being wholly clear what the word meant!) and the way he subsequently sought political allies who would challenge this perception. When I moved to Cheshire CC in the early 1970s, I soon became aware of the different political climate to that of Manchester and the (almost) total domination of Sir John Boynton, the county clerk (as he was then titled) over the political leadership, In the mid-1980s, when based at the Institute of Local Government Studies at the University of Birmingham, I was a member of a research team which carried out a major piece of research into the political organisation of local authorities for the Widdicombe Committee, which involved inter alia, interviews with leaders and chief executives in 103 different local authorities. The mid-1980s was the heyday of the so-called 'loony left' of the Labour party at the local level. Ken Livingstone, Derek Hatton, David Blunkett, Bernie Grant and Graham Stringer were all local leaders characterised (arguably unfairly) by this term, and it was the resistance of the authorities which they led that motivated the Conservative government to set up the Widdicombe Committee. It was a vulnerable time for chief executives, a time when the propensity of 'political logic' and 'managerial logic' to pull in different directions (see Chapter 1) became all too apparent. It has never been easy for ruling parties to dismiss chief executives, but increasingly ways were found of 'easing them out'.

In the late 1990s I carried out research into member–officer relations for the then Local Government Management Board with colleagues at De Montfort University, which produced a further set of insights into the topic. Directors of Social Services were particularly vulnerable at the time, partly because of the propensity of their departments to generate 'bad news' stories. It was also becoming apparent that the increasing number of hung authorities was providing opportunities for 'managerial logic' to dominate, particularly in situations where two of the parties concerned failed to establish a stable joint administration.

The Widdicombe research evidence made it clear that although councils were not required to designate an individual councillor as 'council leader', by 1985 most of them (small rural independent-dominated councils apart) did so. The position of council leader developed in significance in the 1990s and with it the status of the chief executive, whose role began to transcend the familiar traditional 'primus inter pares' label. The election of a Labour government in 1997 and its introduction (in the Local Government Act 2000) of formal local executive government (including the possibility of elected mayors) reinforced this trend. Although officer – member relations has remained an area of interest in its own right, the council leader/chief executive relationship has increased in significance both as a focus of council decision-making and as an area of academic interest. The content of the book I wrote with David Wilson on political leadership[1] reflected these developments. Although the focus was on council leaders, the interviews carried out with them invariably illustrated the growing importance of the leader/chief executive relationship. There were still some ineffective council leaders, who operated as mouthpieces of group opinion and low-profile chief executives who allowed (or were unable to prevent) a high level of autonomy amongst service directors, but they were both increasingly few and far between.

By the time of the next piece of research in which I was involved – a Joseph Rowntree Foundation study of political leadership in England and Wales[2] published in 2005 – the role and status of council leaders and chief executives had been further strengthened by the government's belief in the value of individual leadership, in both spheres, which was expressed in a series of White Papers and other official documents from 2001 onwards and was subsequently reflected in several of the provisions of the Local Government Act 2007 (see Chapter 11). As we shall see, there is little evidential basis for believing that strong individual leadership results in better performance (however measured) than do other more collective styles of leadership. But the re-iteration of the government's belief that it does, coupled with the perspective adopted by the Audit Commission in their corporate assessments of council performance between 2002 and 2008, certainly put pressure on councils to reflect this viewpoint (not least in the carefully rehearsed presentations made to Audit Commission teams during their CPA visits).

The Joseph Rowntree Foundation research carried out in the 2003–2004 period involved in-depth interviews with council leaders and chief executives in nine case-study authorities (three of which had elected mayors) supplemented by similar interviews in seven additional authorities (two of them mayoral). Although the main focus of the research was on political leadership, the detailed notes of the chief executives interviews provided a range of valuable insights into the changing priorities of the chief executive role in the mid-2000s, in particular the impact of the introduction of local executive government, the Audit Commission inspection regime and the ever-increasing emphasis on partnership working.

These notes were a resource I decided I would like to augment and exploit further. In 2007 I successfully applied for a small grant from the Leicester Business School 'seedcorn' research fund, which enabled me to carry out a further 16 interviews with chief executives. It is this material, together with 14 of the interviews with chief executives carried out in connection with the Joseph Rowntree research, which forms the basis for the analysis in this book, although I have also drawn where relevant, on the sequence of earlier research projects outlined above.

The 30 interviewees were not selected at random. The nine case-study authorities in the Joseph Rowntree Foundation research were selected to provide a mix of mayoral authorities (3) and authorities who had adopted the leader and cabinet model (5) plus one 4th option authority. We also ensured that we had a reasonable mix of authority type and political control. The supplementary interviews were carried out in authorities where I have previous contact with the chief executive, and was confident that they would talk frankly to me about their experiences (which indeed they did). Similarly the selection of the 16 chief executives in 2007 was made on the basis of previous knowledge (or in one or two cases, opportunism) for similar reasons. I wanted to avoid situations where interviews might come to be dominated by PR-tinged, 'this is what we have achieved in this authority', types of input, and (with one or two minor exceptions) I am confident that I succeeded in this aim.

In the 2007 interviews I chose not to interview the leaders with whom the chief executives were currently working. I was aware that in the majority of cases, the chief executive concerned had previously held a similar position in one or more other authorities, and I was particularly interested (inter alia) in their comparisons between experiences in their different authorities (and/or where relevant, with different leaders in their current authority). Also I knew I wanted to write a book about the particular experience and perspective of chief executives and, in these circumstances, felt that it was less important to interview leaders also.[3] However, where I felt it was necessary to check out a situation described by a chief executive – particularly in a relationship which had become problematical – I sought informally to do so.

It could be argued that the account I develop in this book about the immersion of chief executives in a political world, and the way they deal with it, is one-sided. Indeed, in Chapter 1, I draw an important distinction between 'political logic' and 'managerial logic' and use it to demonstrate that what makes sense from a political perspective may not do so from a managerial perspective, and vice versa. Thus when in interviews chief executives identified and exemplified 'inappropriate' behaviour on the part of the leader they worked with, such behaviour often (although not always) could be seen as 'appropriate' from the point of view of the leader. A leader who opens a meeting of a Local Strategic Partnership by declaring that the requirement to work in partnership is for him an unwelcome dilution of local democracy and accountability may be sending important signals to his or her party colleagues (as well as no doubt believing it). However, his statement is almost certain to be seen as unhelpful and inappropriate from the managerial perspective of a chief executive, seeking to build bridges with partners.

Indeed, in other places (Leach and Wilson (2000), Gyford, Leach and Game (1989)) I have argued that it is extremely healthy for political leaders to question and challenge the advice they receive from officers (including the chief executive) and to feel free not to take it. Consider some examples; 'leader, there's a wonderful opportunity to solve our housing problem by building high rise flats, and, do you know, the higher we go, the more subsidy we get from the government' or 'leader, I know a lot of residents will be displaced by the Housing Action Area, but we do want a social mix in our inner city areas don't we?' In any major policy dispute between leader and chief executive, my inclination would usually be to side with the former. After all, leaders have a democratic mandate which chief executives lack.

However, this book does not aim to take a balanced view. It is an attempt to understand things from the perspective of chief executives, drawing on in-depth interviews I carried out with 30 of these vulnerable and committed individuals. I do from time to time point out that the managerial viewpoint of a chief executive, quoted in the text, would not necessarily be shared by the political leader involved for legitimate political reasons, to ensure that the reader recognises the need to interpret chief executive perceptions in a wider (political) context. But otherwise I make no apologies for a book which tells the story of operating in a political environment from a chief executives perspective. Anyone seeking a balancing perspective from political leaders can find it elsewhere (Leach and Wilson (2000), Elcock (2001), Leach, Hartley et al. (2005)).

It is worth noting, at this juncture, why in Chapter 1 the literature on leadership has not been given greater prominence. After all, both council leaders and chief executives are indeed 'leaders' in a positional sense, and (in most cases) they exhibit at least some of the qualities typically associated with effective leadership (e.g. decisiveness, responsiveness, charisma, networking capacity etc.). My response is that a review of the vast literature on leadership and the attempt to apply it to the roles and relationships of chief executives would have taken up more space than would have been merited by the 'added value' involved. The crucial aspect of leadership which was highlighted time after time in the insights provided by the chief executives interviewed is one which was used by Leach and Wilson in their book on political leadership (where my views on leadership theory can be reviewed by those interested).

> By leadership behaviour we refer predominantly to explicit actions taken to persuade others... to follow particular lines of action that they would not necessarily be disposed to follow... the essence of leadership is the ability to inspire or persuade others to follow a course of action where there is at least some initial resistance to following it.
>
> (Leach and Wilson 2000, p. 11)

Whatever else leadership involves, it certainly involves the above quality. Leading followers or colleagues who agree with you does not seem to me to require any particular skill. Discovering what the majority of your colleagues think is the right thing to do, and then adopting that as your position is in effect an abdication of leadership. This book focuses (inter alia) on the skills and tactics which are helpful (from a chief executive's perspective) in persuading a leader of the appropriateness of a particular course of action (on the need for a particular change) when the leader is initially unconvinced, or even opposed.

There is much material in this book which will be helpful to new or aspiring chief executives in strengthening their leadership capacity, especially the section of good advice (drawn from the insights of the chief executives interviewed at the end of the book). What is not on offer is yet another book which deals explicitly with leadership theory and leadership skills. There are plenty of those already available!

In the hope of extending the appeal of this book to a wider audience, I have sought to avoid presenting it as an academic treatise. I have used theoretical concepts selectively where I think they will help the reader understand the implications of the empirical material, but there is no comprehensive 'review of the literature' and no attempt to rigorously apply a particular theoretical framework to my findings. Hopefully academic colleagues will accept these limitations and recognise that I wished on this occasion to write a book with a wider appeal.

Of the total of 30 chief executives interviewed, 20 were men and 10 were women. At the time of the interview, six worked in mayoral authorities, 22 in 'leader plus cabinet' authorities and two in 4th option authorities (with 'streamlined committee systems'). Of the authorities concerned seven were shire counties, seven shire districts, three London Boroughs, eight metropolitan boroughs and five unitary authorities. Eight of the councils had a Labour majority, seven a Conservative majority, four a Liberal Democrat majority, ten were hung, and one was dominated by independents. Thus despite the (deliberate) decision not to pursue a random sample, there is clearly a reasonably representative cross-section of authority types and forms of political control in the 30 authorities concerned.

To try to ensure as frank an expression of views from chief executives as possible, I made two commitments. The first was to guarantee anonymity. I am confident that it is not possible to identify any of the chief executives I interviewed within the text of the book (although no doubt some readers will want to hazard guesses). Secondly I decided not to tape record the interviews. Although most of my respondents would have been agreeable to my doing so, my experience in the past is that the presence of a tape recorder does sometimes (not always) have an inhibiting effect, particularly when respondents wish to identify and comment on problematic or dysfunctional behaviour on the part of leaders. As a result, although I have included a large amount of material from the interviews, they are not verbatim quotes. I am confident, however, that my note taking (and retentive memory) means that the words I have used and ascribed to the interviewees concerned represent an accurate sense of the experiences they were describing or points they were making. However, to acknowledge the fact that they are not verbatim quotes, I have distinguished them in the text from the quotes which are verbatim.

The interviews were semi-structured in nature, that is to say there was a list of headings (including one or two specific questions) which I wished to discuss with all the chief executives interviewees. Because the main aim was to encourage chief executives to talk freely about their experiences, the order in which the topics were raised was subject to variation, with a tendency on my part to follow up issues as they emerged from the conversation. I also often responded to points made by interviewees, comparing or contrasting what they said with responses from other chief executives. This may seem to some an unusual way to conduct an interview – indeed the interview often developed into a conversation/discussion – but the device certainly proved helpful in drawing out further justifications (or reservations) from interviewees as to why they had taken a particular stance.

The main focus of the interviews was on the capacity of chief executives to manage within a political environment; hence the emphasis on the relationship with the leader in particular, but also worth key opposition figures. There are of course other important aspects of a chief executive's work – his or her relationship with members of the management team, for example, and the challenge (in many cases) of changing an authority's culture to improve its performance. These 'other aspects' were discussed only in situations where the ability of chief executives to achieve what they wished to achieve had been hampered (or facilitated) by political involvement. For example, a chief executive may see the need for key changes in personnel in the management team which the political leadership may resist. Or attempts to dispel a 'blame culture' may be frustrated by the fact that leading members continue to publicly allocate blame. Such situations are of relevance to this book, but not those which lack any kind of political input (e.g. a 'middle manager' training and development scheme aimed at enhancing organisational capacity or an attempt to rebrand the local authority's image). The book is about the particular challenges facing chief executives in managing in a political environment, not a comprehensive assessment of the overall scope of the job.

My hope is that the book will appeal to two audiences. First academics with an interest in local politics, the strategic management of local authorities and the relationship between political and managerial leaders should find it of interest. As noted, I have not attempted to interpret my findings within any ambitious kind of theoretical framework. However, I have drawn eclectically on various conceptual frameworks which I have found helpful in previous related work, including new institutionalism, leadership task analysis, 'negotiated order' and the use of 'critical incidents'. These approaches are drawn together – albeit relatively loosely – in Chapter 1.

The second target audience is local authority chief executives themselves, and aspirant chief executives. Because the book is based primarily on the practical experience of chief executives in a range of different situations, it contains a good deal of potentially helpful guidance to those who might find themselves in similar situations – for example, 'if you are faced (as I was) with this particular dilemma, here is a way of resolving it'. The book concludes with an extended section of good advice or guidance for chief executives, drawn wholly from the insights and experiences of those interviewed.

Recently (March 2010) chief executives have been in the news, in particular as a result of an Audit Commission report which revealed the size of the pay-offs some of them have recently negotiated when the political leadership had decided they no longer wished to work with them. There has also been increasing speculation about whether the chief executive post, as currently defined, is compatible with the concept of strong political leadership (particularly elected mayors). These topical issues, which are discussed in Chapter 12 may even extend the appeal of the book more widely.

The structure of the book is as follows. Chapter 1 is the conceptual chapter where I set out and discuss the ideas I have found to be helpful in making sense of context in which chief executives operate and the nature of the challenges facing them. I then consider three crucial early stages in a chief executive's experience in a particular authority – deciding whether to apply for a particular job; if offered it, whether or not to accept it; and how to make best advantage of the 'period of grace' or 'honeymoon period' which chief executives almost always experience in the first 6–9 months of a new appointment. There follow three chapters about key aspects of a chief executive's job – the role as head of paid service (in which political leaders are not expected to interfere – but sometimes do); their approach to the absolutely central relationship with the council leader; and the challenge of dealing with political change – particularly a change of administration, but also a change of leader within the same administration. Attention is then focused on the chief executive as a political animal, reflecting the fact that chief executives necessarily become immersed in the world of politics, but the way they deal with this immersion varies considerably, in particular with regard to the 'bottom lines' and 'no go areas' they seek to identify. The essence of a good relationship between a chief executive and political leader is then examined, emphasising the importance of negotiation, whilst critically examining the traditional (but simplistic) view that 'all you need is trust'. In the following chapter, a series of 'critical incidents' which have in one way or another tested the chief executive/leader relationship are elaborated, classified and interpreted. The circumstances in which chief executives have to consider whether they wish to stay in post or seek a job elsewhere are then considered. Two important government initiatives which have profoundly influenced the role of the chief executive and the relationship with political leaders (all party groups) are next discussed; the impact of inspection and the performance culture, and the move to executive government (including the 'special case' of elected mayors). Different future developments in the role of chief executives are then discussed in the light of the research evidence and the changing agenda facing local authorities. Finally a section of 'good advice' distilled from the experiences of the chief executives interviewed is set out.

I would like to express my gratitude to those who were prepared to read through and comment on an earlier draft of this book, in particular Colin Copus, Mark Roberts, Melvin Wingfield and Chris Game. I also acknowledge the influence of a range of other academics who share my interest in the topic covered by this book, and have influenced my thinking about it, notably Vivien Lowndes, David Wilson, Lawrence Pratchett, John Stewart and George Jones. Aileen Kowal has (yet again) coped wonderfully well with the scrawled handwritten versions of my chapters, transforming them into coherence and readability. I am grateful to the Leicester Business School for the seedcorn grant which enabled me to carry out the 16 most recent chief executive interviews, and to the many chief executives who have been prepared to share their thoughts and experiences with me. Finally, thanks again to Karen, Callum and Fergus for providing me with the kind of supportive family environment which makes writing a book like this so much more manageable.

1
Introduction: Understanding the Challenges Facing Chief Executives

A job under pressure?

'Failed chief executives given large payoffs to quit, finds report' was the headline in a recent *Guardian*'s news item (16 March 2010). The report referred to was an Audit Commission publication which had included a number of revelations about such pay-offs including the following:

- Councils had paid an average of £260,000 to 37 chief executives leaving their jobs since 2006.
- The average cost to councils of such payments was 1.8 times the chief executives annual basic salary.
- One chief executive was paid more than £500,000 to leave a job.
- A total of £9.5 million was paid out during the 3-year period of the study.
- One in six of the chief executives who received substantial pay-offs subsequently returned to work in a similar job in a different region.

Some of the reactions reported indicated considerable disquiet at such findings. Bob Neill, the shadow local government minister, regarded such payments as an outrageous waste of taxpayers money; 'there should be no rewards for failure, either in the public or private sector', he said. John Denham, the secretary of state for Communities and Local Government, was somewhat more restrained but agreed that 'too many chief executives are being dismissed because they have fallen out with council leaders...taxpayers money should not be used to resolve personal differences.'

These, and other similar comments, represent simplistic responses to a complex problem. A more balanced analysis of the issue of pay-offs for unwanted chief executives is provided in Chapter 12. However, the fact that just over one-third of chief executives who left their jobs between 2006 and 2009 did so unwillingly and ended up negotiating substantial severance packages indicates that the problems facing chief executives in 'managing in a political environment' have resulted in an increased vulnerability for holders of such positions.

Anyone seeking confirmation of this trend could have found it in many of the headlines of the *Local Government Chronicle* (*LGC*) and *Municipal Journal* (*MJ*) during the 2001–2009 period. Here are some typical examples.

> Kingston Chief takes charge as political leadership crumbles (*MJ* 22 March 2002)
> New Liverpool leader 'unsure' about Henshaw (*MJ* 8 December 2005)
> Lincs Tories block return of whistle-blower Bowles (*LGC* 23 April 2004)
> Council 'jumps gun' on ousted chief (Cheltenham BC) (*MJ* 11 August 2005)
> 'Friends' united: Islington leader and chief executive grilled over relationship (*MJ* 13 October 2005).

The issue is raised of whether these problematic situations represent the 'tip of the iceberg', or alternatively, the inevitability of the occasional breakdown of relationships when there are around 400 different local authorities in England. If it were the first conclusion which was accurate, then anyone writing a book about chief executives would have material for a best seller. However, the view that the second conclusion might have some substance is borne out by a second set of headlines – typically attached to articles rather than news stories – from the same publications.

'Working in Harmony' (LB Ealing's Chief Executive and its new leader discuss the qualities of their relationship) (*MJ* 6 July 2006)

'Magic Wand' (LB Wandsworth's Chief Executive and leader are asked about the secret of their success) (*MJ* 10 August 2006)

'Building on Sound Foundations' (Telford and Wrekin's Chief Executive believes in finishing what you start) (*LGC* 20 February 2004).

Not surprisingly, the reality lies somewhere between the 'tip of the iceberg' and 'conflict as exception' perceptions. Of the 30 chief executives interviewed in connection with this book, about one-fifth were experiencing (or had recently experienced) long-term problematic relationships with their leaders, about two-fifths were extremely positive about their relationship, whilst the remainder were managing reasonably satisfactorily, but with areas of disagreement or occasional crises which had proved difficult to resolve. Whilst not claiming representativeness for the 30 chief executives concerned, previous research suggests that this is not an untypical pattern of experiences (see, e.g. Leach, Pratchett and Wingfield 1997). The reality is that relationships between chief executives and leaders are neither inherently problematical nor inherently straightforward. As we shall see, much depends on the ability of the two leading figures to negotiate a mutually acceptable way of working.

What the various headlines quoted above illustrate (as does much else that has been written about in the role of the chief executive since 2000) is the crucial importance of the relationship the chief executive has with the leader in enabling him or her to 'do a good job' (we will return to what 'doing a good job' involves shortly). There are of course other important relationships in a chief executive's working life, for example those with members of the authority's management team, with opposition leaders, and with heads of key partner organisations. But the relationship with the council leader provides a focus for the chief executive's agenda, and a context for his or her other relationships. The significance of the relationship has increased steadily over the past decade, as political leadership has become more formalised and individualised. Whether consensual, unpredictable or problematical, the relationship with the leader is a key factor in understanding in the capacity of the chief executive to respond to the strategic agenda (as he or she sees it) facing the authority. As Islington's former chief executive Eric Dear put it:

> It is vital that the leader and the chief executive are seen to be on the same side and that it is the winning side. In my view the council cannot work effectively unless the leader and chief executive understand and complement each other and respect and are comfortable with each other. If they are not and cannot reach that position, then one of them needs to move on.

Geoff Filkin, when chief executive of Reading, emphasised that 'the leader has a role in affirming the chief executive's responsibility over chief officers and their services'. Reciprocity is the order of the day. As Camden's chief executive saw it, 'you are the political interface, particularly with the leader', a point emphasised by Coventry's chief executive in 1997, Ian Roxburgh: 'The relationship between chief executive and leader shapes the way the authority is run. I wouldn't have a job if I didn't think I could work with the leader.'[1]

Institutions, rules and roles

What kind of conceptual framework is most appropriate for a book which focuses on chief executives, the challenges they face in operating in a political environment, and in particular on their relationship with political leaders?

In previous work by the author and colleagues the importance of two such frameworks has been postulated and exemplified: first an approach known as 'new institutionalism' and second, an identification of the generic leadership tasks which face local authorities. The value of these two frameworks of analysis is justified below.

Leach (2006, p. 8) argues that one starting point is to emphasise the kind of framework that is *not* felt to be appropriate. Underpinning a range of central government initiatives has been the assumption that by changing organisational and political *structures*, you can change behaviour. Thus, if you want to achieve 'strong leadership' in local government, then what you do is introduce new structures – for example, elected mayors – which enhance the formal powers of leaders. At worst, this kind of approach degenerates into a form of structural determinism. Even if not reaching this extreme, the approach typically gives more weight to the importance of changes in structures and 'legal requirements' than is actually merited.

In reality, new structures, legal requirements and government expectations, imposed from outside, impinge upon a set of cultural values and working practices, often long established, about 'the way things are done here'. The importance of the cultural context into which new structures and requirements are interpreted is the essence of a conceptual framework known as 'new institutionalism'. 'New institutionalism' highlights the importance of culture context, roles and 'rules of the game'. Lowndes (2004, p. 234) provides a helpful explanation of the main features of this approach.

> Organisations – like individuals – are players within that game. In urban politics, relevant 'rules' may be consciously designed and clearly specified – like constitutions and structure plans, community strategies, or performance plans and agreements. Alternatively rules may take the form of unwritten customs and codes. Informal rules may support 'positive' patterns of behaviour, like 'community leadership', the 'public service ethos' or 'continuous improvement'; or they may underpin 'negative' frameworks like departmentalism, paternalism or social exclusion. The players within the 'game' of local governance are diverse, and include organisations (the elected local authority, other service agencies, political parties, voluntary organisations) and individuals (politicians, bureaucrats, service professionals, community activists, electors).

New institutionalism is not a causal theory, but rather a broad conceptual framework whose value lies in provoking 'questions that might occur' and in producing 'new and fresh insights' (Judge, Stoker and Wolman 1995, p. 3). The 'new institutional' framework enables us to explore the relationship between structure, context and agency at the apex of local authorities where political and managerial leadership intermesh. Lowndes and Leach (2004) identified three basic propositions about the relevance of institutions in this setting.

- Local political institutions have both formal and informal dimensions: change is shaped by their complex interaction and the tenacity of informal elements.
- Local political institutions are embedded in wider institutional frameworks: change is shaped by institutional constraints in the external political environment and within specific local contexts.
- Local political institutions have meaning and effect only through the actions of individuals: change is a creative, negotiated and contested process

(Lowndes and Leach 2004, pp. 561–563).

Although the term 'political' is used in the quote, these propositions are equally applicable to managerial institutions in local government. These three propositions highlight the importance of *negotiation* between key individuals (in this case chief executives and leaders) in making judgements about how to respond to the range of different challenges facing an authority. In that process of negotiation, skills (or capabilities) may play an important part in deciding outcomes. For example, a persuasive chief executive, with the ability to present arguments in terms which are sensitive to the political ideology of the leader, is more likely to achieve desired outcomes than one who lacks this skill. Such 'attempts to persuade' may, however, come up against the tenacity of long-established institutional elements. For example, the 2000 Local Government Act was intended to sweep away or at least minimise a number of traditional practices. Yet many of these practices proved remarkably resilient.

> Traditionally, political behaviour on local councils has been shaped by the formal rules and informal conventions associated with the party group and the committee system, expressed in such features as the cycle of meetings, standing orders, pre-meetings of group members and expectations about the role of chair, majority party and opposition (which John Stewart, 2000, p. 43, has identified as the 'ingrained committee habit'). One conclusion that has been emphasised in numerous research papers on the operation of the new political management structure is the survival of this 'ingrained committee habit' in the context where it is usually less than appropriate to the functions involved (in particular to the role of overview and scrutiny).
>
> (Leach 2006, pp. 9–10)

It is not being argued that externally-imposed structures and legal requirements do not make some difference. They clearly do. Legal requirements have to be met, but typically leave a good deal of 'scope for interpretation'. New structures provide opportunities, and sometimes justifications, for individuals or groups to strengthen their influence on decision-making, but such opportunities can also be reduced by constitutional provisions or informal traditions or may not be exploited if the incumbent lacks the capacity to do so.

The importance of actors (or agents) in shaping the change and the stories actors tell about 'the way we do things here' are important features of new institutionalism. Roberts and Leach (2010) identify three further (interrelated) features of new institutionalism which are relevant to the roles and relationships of chief executives.

> Firstly, institutions embody ideas and, in public policy and political analysis, ideas are powerful weapons in the hands of political and managerial actors. Institutions express a particularly potent set of ideas which not only constrain, but also empower, actors. Institutions limit the choices available to actors but, in freeing them from infinite choice, also free them to act. Furthermore, the ways in which institutions are designed, applied and interpreted in the public policy arena define who is included and excluded, and who has a say and who does not.
>
> Secondly, institutions are the rules which shape the everyday behaviour of political and managerial actors. They take on various forms as, for example, the formal rules which first spring to mind when the term 'rule' is used, but they also appear as the informal rules of conduct in any given context, which are usually unwritten, but exert a strong influence on actors' thinking and action. In their wider manifestations, institutions take the form of stories which tell actors about 'the way we do things around here'. In these narrative accounts which relate details of the local political context, the expression of the rule usually comes at the end of the story as a normative conclusion, or moral, which tells actors how things have been done in the past and how they should be done in the future.
>
> Finally, institutions appear to be stable and durable. This appearance of stasis is created by the interlinkages made and maintained

by actors between these formal, informal and narrative layers which preserve their general shape over long periods. But beneath this veneer institutions are only 'relatively' stable. This tension between stability and change is caused by the dialectic relationship with actors in which 'the rules of the game' both influence, and are themselves influenced by, the conduct of those actors.

(Roberts and Leach 2010, forthcoming)

All the key features of new institutionalism, including its emphasis on actors' roles, rules (formal and informal), agency, stories, negotiated order, context, culture and capabilities, can be applied with advantage to an analysis of relationships between chief executives and political leaders. The approach provides an essential balance to an (over)emphasis on formal structures and legal requirements, without denying the significance of both of these influences.

There are several distinctive features of the political and organisational culture of local authorities which make the application of a new institutionalist perspective particularly relevant. In particular:

- Chief executives are increasingly expected (not least by the government) to demonstrate qualities of leadership, but each does so within a specific range of constraints.
- Chief executives are expected to form 'good relationships' with leading politicians and to work closely with them, but do so on the basis of different rationalities and rules of the game (managerial logic differs from political logic, as is discussed later in the chapter).
- The context in which each local authority operates is distinctive, and hence presents distinctive challenges to chief executives (and political leaders). There are wide variations in the mix of social, economic and environmental problems faced by local authorities; in their political cultures and traditions (including inter-party relationships) and in their constitutions, which set out in formal terms the division of responsibilities between executives, the council and chief officers (including chief executives) respectively.
- Much of the managerial and political activity undertaken in local authorities has to be undertaken collectively. Although the individual leadership role of chief executives and council leaders has been increasingly emphasised since 2000, the reality is that there

are limits to what can be decided by chief executives and council leaders individually (or together). It is generally necessary to build coalition support from proposals emanating from these sources, using persuasion and negotiation drawing on informal norms of 'the way we do business in this authority'.

In these circumstances, structural explanations of outcomes have only a limited applicability. If the new executive structures introduced by the Local Government Act 2000 had proved a decisive influence on chief executive's roles and their relationships with leading politicians, one would have expected a much greater uniformity in the pattern of roles and relationships which developed. In reality, although some general trends resulting from the introduction of local executive structures can be identified (see Chapter 11), the variety of outcomes is much more striking than the common features, even amongst mayoral authorities. Lowndes and Leach (2004) discuss the relative significance of context, constitutions and capabilities in the interpretation of political and managerial leadership, and conclude that context and capabilities are just as significant in explaining patterns of political and managerial leadership (and their interactions) as constitutions (which embody the formal structural changes), often more so. Leach and Lowndes (2007) identify a series of informal 'rules of the game' which have developed and significantly influenced chief executive/leader relationships (with significant variations of interpretation) within local authorities since 2000.

All these key features of the way of working of local authorities since 2000, in particular the importance of context (especially political culture), the formal and informal 'rules of the game', and the capabilities (including negotiating and coalition building skills) of key actors, are central to the framework of analysis provided by new institutionalism. Due weight is accorded to the influence of agency (or key actors) operating within a context of formal and informal rules and procedures, which can be changed, but often only with considerable difficulty.

Political logic and managerial logic

In applying the concepts of new institutionalism to local government, an important distinction has to be made between local authorities and other sub-national public agencies. The former are unique in that they are led by a group of directly elected councillors with political values and political careers (unlike the board members of other local public sector agencies).

Listening to leaders and chief executives discussing their relationships, one sometimes gets a strong sense that the main ingredients of a 'good relationship' are *personal qualities* – such as mutual trust, respect and the ability to communicate effectively – and a *sense of common purpose* – such as partnership, shared objectives and 'the good of the authority'. The crucial nature of the political/managerial distinction is not always readily apparent.

There is no reason to doubt the sincerity of the sentiments expressed. These qualities can be seen as essential conditions for good political management in an authority. If an authority, as an entity, has a clear sense of purpose and set of objectives, a strategic vision to which members and officers are equally committed, and a shared set of understandings about the way the authority should operate, and if the leader and chief executive (and portfolio holders and directors) have developed good personal relationships, then both officers and members have an invaluable basis for responding to the challenges facing them.

There are however two reasons why an overemphasis on good personal relations and shared objectives can become detrimental to an understanding of the dynamics of leader/chief executive relations. As Leach, Pratchett and Wingfield (1997, p. 9) argue

> First, too much emphasis on what is shared can hide or marginalise the reality that members and officers come to local authorities with very different personal, political and professional goals and agendas. For example ad hoc departures from the policy planning/budgeting allocations system in the year before a local election may be illogical and disturbing to a chief executive, but entirely justifiable from the perspective of a majority group faced with an election. Managerial and political logic sometimes point in different directions. Second, too much emphasis on common purpose can hide or diminish an awareness of the need for clear definitions of the distinctive roles of members and officers respectively in achieving that common purpose. Such definitions may operate on an informal rather than a formal basis, but they are

an essential element in avoiding many of the major sources of misunderstanding, tension or conflict between members and officers. The blurring of roles is, we found, a recipe for problems and sometimes disaster in member-officer relations.

The key point to emphasise is that there are major differences of perspective between councillors and officers (and between leaders and chief executives). These differences stem largely from the reliance of the former, but not the latter, on election (and re-election) as a necessary condition for their presence in the council. This sounds like an uncontentious truism, but profound consequences flow from it. Party groups are concerned to maximise their chances of electoral success, that is, to achieve or retain majority control, or if that is unrealistic to increase their representation and influence (e.g. in a balanced or hung authority). It follows that the performance of the party, as perceived by the public, will be a crucial concern for local politicians, because of its potential effect on future electoral success. Officers, on the other hand, are appointed rather than elected and will typically bring to their role a set of professional and/or managerial values which may in certain circumstances clash with the political values (and political expedients) of councillors.

Thus one key starting point for any realistic in-depth analysis of councillor–officer relationships must be the differences between on the one hand (party) political perspectives and on the other managerial/professional perspectives. Relevant skills (leadership, consensus-seeking, honesty) may help to manage tensions which arise from the fact that these two perspectives pull in different directions, but they cannot (and should not) seek to ignore or marginalise the sources of these tensions. Similarly, structural forms (e.g. executive government, see Chapter 11) and process constraints (e.g. the Comprehensive Performance Assessment (CPA), see Chapter 10) provide contexts in which these tensions are more or less likely to arise and also contexts in which they have to be resolved.

Identifying underlying council objectives

It is difficult and indeed counterproductive to seek to identify characteristics of a 'good' relationship between chief executives and leaders without first establishing what it is good *for*. As discussed above, politicians and officers operate in a local authority with different objectives and expectations, stemming from the different reasons they have for being there. Politicians are there primarily to achieve political ends, and to seek to achieve or sustain a level of political power within an authority that enables them to achieve, at least partially, those ends (e.g. majority control may be out of the reach of a smaller party, but not membership for a ruling coalition).

Officers are there at particular stages in their careers, and would normally seek to display professional and/or managerial abilities in a way which provides a basis for further career progression. There is an important difference between professional and managerial objectives. The professional perspective will typically include a desire to implement whatever professional ideas are currently in good currency (e.g. for a town planner, at various times in the past, high rise flats, inner ring roads, neighbourhood units and new towns), ideas which may or may not be valued by the politicians when they advise. The managerial perspective will typically seek to apply whatever ideas of good management are currently in vogue (e.g. performance measurement, mission statements, customer-orientation) particularly those which are subject to external identification and evaluation, as in the CPA system.

How can these different perspectives be brought together? The centrality of purpose (or objectives) in the analysis of leadership behaviour has been emphasised by Clarence Stone.

> Leadership revolves around purpose and purpose is at the heart of the leader-follower relationship. Indeed, in some cases, a compelling statement of mission not only gives direction to a group... but shapes the identity of group members by highlighting a shared aim.
>
> (Stone 1995, pp. 96–97)

How then can the key purposes of local authorities which transcend authority type, political control and political managerial value differences be characterised? Leach and Wilson (2000, p. 14) in their study of political leadership note that task-oriented leadership is a well-developed field of study in organisational behaviour. Selznick identifies four functions of institutional leadership: the definition of institutional mission and role; the institutional embodiment of purpose; the defence of institutional integrity; and the ordering of internal conflict (Selznick 1957). However, these headings were intended as a general perspective for the study of leadership in any administrative organisation, and require modification in the specific situation of a political organisation such as a local authority.

In the Kotter and Lawrence (1974) study of elected mayors, six behavioural models of political leadership are identified of which the authors argue two are concerned primarily with the setting of policy, two with its execution and two with organisation and service management. They are thus able to identify three key mayoral processes: agenda setting, task accomplishment and network-building and maintenance. Game (1979) argued that these distinctions formed an appropriate basis for studying leadership in British local government. Leach and Wilson (2000) conclude that if the last process – network-building and maintenance – is subdivided into *internal* (maintaining cohesiveness) and *external* (representing the authority in the outside world) elements, then we have a categorisation of leadership tasks that is particularly helpful in the British context. These tasks can be summarised as maintaining organisational cohesiveness, developing strategic direction, representing the authority in the outside world and ensuring programme implementation (Leach and Wilson 2000, p. 14).

> Of these four key tasks (or purposes) 'maintaining organisational cohesiveness' (or 'ensuring a stable and supportive decision-making environment') may be regarded as secondary to the other three (although it is of crucial importance). 'Providing a clear strategic direction', 'using external networks to further the authority's priorities' and 'ensuring good performance' are directly concerned with the way in which an authority deals with the substantive agenda of needs, problems and duties facing it 'Ensuring a stable and supportive decision-making environment' is concerned with the kind of organisational culture needed to achieve these primary objectives.

Interestingly, these four tasks provide the focus for much of the Audit Commission's assessment of the corporate performance of local authorities.[2] The fact that the Audit Commission has been so concerned in its reviews about an authority's priorities, corporate strategy, partnership working, service delivery and also, indeed, about key aspects of its political/organisational culture, has highlighted the importance of these overriding tasks to political and managerial leaders alike, whereas previously the recognition of their significance had often been less explicit.

The four key tasks are all highly relevant to the agendas of both political and managerial leaders. They all provide scope for different views as to what is an appropriate division of political/managerial responsibilities. Dealing with these 'division of labour' issues is a crucial element of a chief executive's job. Indeed, as we shall see, disagreements about 'who does what' have been the cause of major problems in the relationship, sometimes resulting in an impasse or breakdown in relationships which have made it difficult for a chief executive to continue in post. The scope for disagreements within each key task is illustrated below. A chief executive who can negotiate with a leader a division of responsibilities which enables him or her (as a manager) to achieve good performance (however defined), and to overcome a range of potential political constraints or barriers to doing so, is in a fortunate position indeed.

Ensuring a stable and supportive decision-making environment

The complexity of a local authority as a politically led multi-purpose agency means that this task has a number of different elements. As far as the political dimension is concerned, if there is a majority party then the leadership will clearly wish to sustain the cohesiveness of the party group (and the cabinet from which it is drawn); and if schisms or factionalism exist within the group, the leadership wishes to manage them effectively (and certainly to ensure that they do not affect the public face of the council). If the authority is hung then there will be an inter-party dimension to this leadership task; maintaining a working relationship with the other party or parties who are co-operating with the council leadership, either through a coalition or in supporting a minority administration. The chief executive will be concerned to ensure that the management team operates as a collectivity, responsive to his or her leadership, and which avoids the 'silo culture' characteristics which were (and sometimes still are) characteristic of officer structures. Finally there is the task (for which leader and chief executive together are primarily responsible), of ensuring that members and officers can work together in a cohesive way (whilst acknowledging their different roles). In principle, one would expect the political dimension to be the responsibility of the council leader, the managerial dimension to be that of the chief executive, and the member–officer interface to be a joint leader/chief executive responsibility. As will become apparent, however, it is by no means unusual for chief executives to be drawn into the task of securing or maintaining political cohesiveness.

Providing a clear strategic direction

There is in all local authorities a leadership task of strategy/policy initiation or agenda setting. (What kind of authority are we? Where are we going? What kind of policy should we have in relation to economic development?) This task, which is more explicit and better developed in some authorities than in others, is of growing importance in a world of 'community governance' and financial constraint. It is a task that may be exercised proactively or reactively (as in a crisis). The necessity to carry out this task explicitly has been strengthened by the expectations involved in the Audit Commission-led CPA process. The political starting point for strategy would be the content of the most recent party manifesto, with whatever additions have been developed to cope with unforeseen circumstances. The managerial dimension would involve the chief executive's judgement as to the form and content of a strategy which would be acceptable to external inspection (e.g. the CPA). Clearly there is a good deal of scope for interpretation and negotiation between the political and managerial viewpoints, with the added complication of a political wish in certain circumstances (particularly in the run-up to an election) to 'keep options open', a desire which may not be compatible with a strategy which embodies selective priorities.

Using external networks to further the authority's priorities

This leadership task has increased in significance in recent years. Local authorities now have to work with a range of other organisations to achieve their objectives. The fragmented structure of community governance means that, on many of the issues facing local authorities, they are in partnership with other public bodies. This means that it is important for both political and managerial leaders to maintain contacts with a wide range of individuals and organisations in establishing the role of the local authority in community leadership. The importance of the task has been accentuated by the focus on the way authorities handle partnership working in the CPA process. Again there is an important issue of the division of responsibilities for this task between the chief executive (and his or her senior colleagues) and the council leader (and his or her cabinet colleagues). Should the leader or the chief executive chair the Local Strategic Partnership? The Local Crime and Disorder Partnership? How are relationships with the media to be dealt with and by whom?

Ensuring good performance and the delivery of priorities

Although in most textbooks this task is conventionally delegated to officers ('members make policy; officers implement it'), in many politicised authorities the division of labour is not seen in such cut-and-dried terms. Although there are clearly limits to the extent to which local politicians can 'ensure delivery' (through limitations of time, if nothing else), there is now a widespread, though contested, acceptance of the principle that politicians have a legitimate interest in task accomplishment (i.e. in ensuring that what they want to happen does happen). The legitimacy of this interest applies particularly to elected mayors who may be judged, when standing for re-election, on the basis of their record of delivering what they promised. Thus, as with the other organisational tasks, there is a political and a managerial dimension, with a potential area of tension at the interface. As we shall see, the involvement of some leaders in micromanagement has been a major cause for concern for the chief executives involved.

The key argument here is that whatever differences there are between political objectives and professional priorities, there will be a common interest amongst councillors and officers to ensure that the local authority has a clear sense of direction (or priorities), is able to ensure that it delivers what it set out to deliver and that it maximises its influence in dealings with external agencies to achieve its priorities. It would be widely recognised that a stable and cohesive organisational environment (including the councillor/officer interface) is a necessary (though not sufficient) condition for achieving the first three objectives.

As we have noted there is a wide scope for discussion about the division of responsibilities between members and officers in seeking to achieve each of these four objectives; and there may be circumstances where organisational stability is very difficult to achieve, hence jeopardising the achievement of the other objectives. But they will always be important reference points for analysing councillor officer relations. Their importance has been highlighted by the priority given to strategy, service delivery, performance management and partnership working in the CPA system.

Learning from other types of leader/chief executive relationship

The academic literature on leader/chief executive relationships is patchy and there is little that addresses the profound changes since 2000 in the context in which council leaders and chief executives operate. Cabinet government (and elected mayors), CPAs, and the increased emphasis on partnership working and public involvement have all had major consequences for the relationship. The most helpful contributions which take into account such developments are those by Gains (2004) and Fox, Skelcher and Lyons (2002).

There are also potential lessons which can be learned from studies of other comparable (but different) relationships, namely,

- chairmen of the board and managing directors in private sector organisations
- chairs of quangos (and non-elected public sector bodies) and chief executives thereof
- government ministers and senior civil servants.

Private sector

However in each case, particularly the first, the relevance of findings to local government is limited by the differences in the context within which the relationships operate. In the private sector managing directors are invariably members of the board, unlike chief executives who (except in the one-off case of Stoke-on-Trent) are not. In addition, the objectives of private sector organisations are predominantly profit- and growth-oriented with managing directors expected to deliver within relatively clearly-defined and measurable parameters. In common with Ranson and Stewart's seminal work (1994) a review of the literature on chairman/managing director relationships provided few insights into the challenges of the chief executive/council leader relationship. The SOLACE report (2006) presented a similar view.

> There are no direct comparisons with the private sector, where the relationship between a chief executive and a company's board is entirely different, and less transparent than in a council. In the private sector non-executive responsibilities are prescribed in company law....
>
> (SOLACE 2006, p. 11)

Public sector

Literature on the relationship between chairs of the boards (or whatever) of other public sector organisations (e.g. housing associations, PCTs, Hospital Trusts) and their chief executives is somewhat more rewarding. Some of the emergent conclusions have a degree of relevance to an understanding of chief executive/council leader relationship:

> i. It would be a mistake to pay so much attention to the often part-time appointed members if it is the full-time professional officers who exert most influence on the management of local public spending bodies.
>
> (Greer and Hoggett 1997, p. 215)

> ii. However, the overwhelming impression obtained from the case studies of housing associations and further education colleges is not one of board member intrusion into the sphere of management but of the primacy of management in setting the strategic direction of the organisation. Typically strategic issues are first flagged and are then presented to boards as strategic items for discussion, often at board away-days. In such circumstances, is the role of the board simply that of the 'rubber stamp'? By and large we would say no, or at least, not quite. Many members saw the role of the board in terms of subjecting management proposals

to detailed scrutiny, offering different perspectives, providing a context, acting as a 'back stop' etc.

(Greer and Hoggett 1997, p. 217)

iii. Although mutual trust and co-operation are essential between the chair and the chief executive, the responsibilities of the two are different and distinct. One is about direction and the other about management. It is important that there is a close working relationship but neither should try to do the job of the other.... The chief executive must play a full part in helping the board to develop the strategy, policies and reputation of the association. The board, in turn, should support the chief executive but must be firmly discouraged from discussing day to day management issues which are the chief executive's responsibility, except insofar as they involve questions of policy or reputation.

(NFHA 1995, p. 31)

iv. The roles of chairs (of Registered Social Landlords) and chief executives were seen as broadly distinct although in some cases they did overlap, but with few apparent serious consequences. Activities involving external partners was one area which caused some role uncertainties.

(Exworthy 2000)

v. Both chairman and general manager (of Health Authorities) have a distinctive domain... the chairman for example must chair the authority meetings and the general manager must brief the chairman beforehand and must supervise members of the management team... both have domains that would normally be considered theirs, but where the other may choose to get involved... or may feel called upon to because the other is not doing so.

(Stewart 1999)

All these quotes reflect situations which can be found in local authorities. The first two might apply to relatively unpoliticised or politically disorganised authorities, where chief executives typically dominate the agenda at the political/managerial leadership interface, including (as in the second quote) a de facto role of setting the council's strategic priorities. The third quote puts in a nutshell the 'ideal relationship' between the chief executive and the political leadership but one which is much harder to achieve in local authorities than in other public sector organisations. The two final quotes indicate that 'who does what' issues – particularly in relation to partnership working – was an issue for other public sector organisations, as it can be in local authorities.

However, the parallels can only be taken so far. Chairs of such boards are in a much weaker position than council leaders. In discussions/negotiations with their chief executives they (usually) lack the detailed knowledge that their counterparts have *and* they lack the legitimacy (and accountability) which council leaders have in asserting what should be achieved and (to an extent) how it should be achieved. They lack the popular mandate which would justify them in challenging managerial advice. To quote the SOLACE report again

> …in other public service organisations, none have the complexity of producing such a wide range of highly visible public services, nor the combination of local media interest, constant political criticism and such high levels of transparency and public accountability. Chief executives of local authorities unlike those in the private sector or other public sector agencies are not voting members of an executive board.
>
> (SOLACE 2006, p. 11)

One's overall impression is that chairs of quangos and so on often act as public spokespersons for a managerially dominant agenda which they have little choice but to accept. There are exceptions particularly where the chair has a body of prior experience elsewhere in relation to the key tasks of the organisation. However, more common is an inequality in the relationship with the balance of effective power with the chief executive, much more so than is generally the case with council leader/chief executive relationships (although there have been cases where council leaders have largely become to a large extent 'spokespersons for a managerial direction').

Ministers and civil servants

There are more parallels in the third comparative area – ministers/civil servants. A trawl through episodes of the 'Yes Minister' and 'Yes

Prime Minister' series reveals several similarities with the operation of leader/chief executive relationships. Like chief executives, senior civil servants have their own policy preferences, whatever they may claim about being there to serve ministers' wishes. The pro-Europe stance of the Foreign Office throughout the years of doubt in the later stages of the 1979–1997 period of Conservative government is well-documented. The importance of negotiation skills is apparent in both cases. No doubt there have been many examples of council leaders looking aghast when told by chief executives what a 'brave' decision they are contemplating! The scope for different 'balances of power' in the minister/civil servant relationship depending on how strong (or weak) the minister is also has parallels in local government.

However, there are also important differences which limit the scope of the comparison. First, senior civil servants' role responsibility is to the government of the day; they are not obliged to serve the Parliament (unlike the way chief executives are required in principle to 'serve the whole council').[3] Thus the need to take account of the views of opposition members and backbench members of the governing party is not an issue for civil servants (unlike chief executives). Secondly the link between minister and permanent secretary has been considerably affected in recent years by the growth of special advisors (and media-management personnel) who provide alternative sources of policy advice. This process is not replicated in local government (except perhaps in the GLA). Very few authorities have taken advantage of the power to appoint political advisors; and where they have done so, it has been in the knowledge that such appointments are required to be at a relatively junior level. Thirdly ministers are rarely required to refer things back to the Parliamentary party (the equivalent of the party group in local authorities) whilst for a council leader, the views of the group are still likely to be a major concern (or if the authority is hung, the views of the other party leaders). Fourthly, much of the delivery of central government policies is now in the hands of 'arms length' agencies or quangos, which makes it much more difficult (although not impossible) for ministers to become involved in micromanagement (if they were to be so inclined). And finally dismissing civil servants is virtually impossible!

The overall conclusion which emerges from this set of comparisons is that the differences between chief executive/council leader relationships and similar pairings in the private sector and elsewhere in the public sector are more striking than the similarities. As a result, the set of challenges facing chief executives in their requirement to 'manage in a political environment' are distinctive and in some cases unique to their particular role. Some interesting comparisons have been drawn (more so in the public than the private sector). But there is little value (for the purposes of this book) in creating an elaborate analytical framework based on such comparisons.

The dimensions of a good relationship

What is meant by identifying the relationship between chief executive and leader in a particular authority as 'good' (or 'poor' or 'indifferent')? The obvious (though, in reality, inadequate) starting point is to look at the qualities of the relationship in personal terms. Is it consensual or conflictual? Are there high levels of trust, respect and honesty in the relationship? Is there a sense of partnership and common purpose? If relationship is imbued with the kind of positive qualities identified above, then presumably it can be characterised in positive terms – that is, as 'good'?

The problem with this perspective, as already noted, is that a 'good' relationship (as characterised in these terms) can co-exist with a situation of officer domination, where the strategic agenda of the authority is in reality set by the chief executive and the senior management (who also have clear and exclusive responsibility for implementing it). Leading members may well be happy to take credit for the council's achievement (e.g. a good or excellent CPA rating) even when they have contributed little to it. There is an important sense in which a relationship cannot be seen as good if it is dominated by officers. The point is equally valid if it is members who dominate the relationship. It is possible to imagine a situation in which member domination has become an established element of a local authority's culture, and because officers have come to accept it as 'inevitable', it operates in an environment of consensus and amicable personal relations (though probably not honesty or mutual respect!) If the relationship lacks a major political input into strategy or lacks a capacity for officers to challenge the priorities of members (at least in terms of making clear their views about possible negative impacts) then it cannot be sensibly characterised as 'good'.

It follows that there is (much) more to a 'good' relationship than consensual amicable personal relations between chief executives and leaders. It should be emphasised that a consensual relationship, warmly regarded from both sides, is not necessarily an effective one (see Chapter 7). One chief executive enjoyed, on the face of it, a very good relationship with her leader, but it was very much on her terms, with her playing the dominant role, which is not necessarily a desirable situation from a political perspective. Other chief executives had the kind of relationship with their leaders that incorporated periodic explosive disagreements, but recognised that this style of operation was actually helpful in resolving problems and was not detrimental to the overall quality of the relationship. Style should not be mistaken for substance; nor consensus for democratic viability.

Some kind of appropriate balance has to be achieved between political priorities and managerial/professional advice, not least about the feasibility of the implementation of such priorities, and the need to take account of their consequences for the status and reputation of the authority (e.g. in relation to CPA inspections) or the likely impact on the local population (or particular groups within it).

In an authority where a reasonable balance has been achieved between political and managerial/professional perspectives and there exist mechanisms for resolving conflicts which result from differences in these perspectives, the quality of the councillor/officer relationship may be far from consensual or amicable. It may be, at times, challenging (from both directions) or even acrimonious ('are you really telling me there is no legal way we can implement our policy?)'. But if the various actors accept this way of working as necessary or appropriate as a way of resolving differences, and if the challenging exchanges take place within an atmosphere of trust openness and mutual respect (and no hard feelings remain once an issue has been resolved) then the relationship could reasonably be characterised as 'good'.

There is a further important dimension to a (genuinely) 'good' relationship that there is a clear mutually acceptable and appropriate division of labour between councillors and officers. The relevant starting point here is the four overreaching objectives of local authorities identified earlier. There are many different formulae for dividing responsibilities for achieving their objectives. Some would be quite inappropriate (e.g. officers set the strategy; members seek to deliver services; or officers take a leading role in seeking to establish a stable and cohesive political culture). But there is a range of different possibilities that, in particular circumstances, may be seen as appropriate (or at least 'not inappropriate'). Officers may contribute proactively to a discussion about strategic priorities. Cabinet members may choose to extend their executive decision-making responsibilities to a level which goes well below that of 'key decisions'. Chief executives may act as a broker to help form an administration in an authority that moves from majority control to 'no overall control'. Lead responsibilities in the various partnerships a local authority is involved in may be allocated between councillors and officers in a range of different ways. There are few hard and fast rules. The important condition is that the division of responsibilities should be transparent (with a degree of flexibility and a good deal of consultation) and well-understood on both sides.

The antithesis of this situation, a blurring of roles and responsibilities (or an inappropriate division) is not compatible with a 'good' relationship, even if it operates in a consensual and amicable climate. That is the danger in a local authority which emphasises characteristics of partnership, common interests and claims that 'we are all working for the good of the community here'. That may well be so; but unless it is clear what the distinctive political inputs are to the achievement of that worthy aim, and where political responsibility ceases and managerial responsibility takes over, there exist the seeds of internal malfunctioning and diminished public accountability.

On the basis of the arguments set out above, a 'good' chief executive/leader relationship would be one which was 'fit for purpose' at three different levels.

(1) A transparent, mutually understood and mutually accepted and appropriate division of roles and responsibilities between councillors and officers.
(2) A set of mechanisms for exposing and resolving the differences of judgement and priority that will inevitably arise from the different perspectives of politicians and managers respectively.
(3) A set of personal relationships which embody the qualities of honesty, openness and trust and which facilitate processes of challenge (and occasional explicit and heated disagreement)

without damaging the ability of the actors concerned to work together effectively.

Although all these characteristics are important, in the absence of both of the first two levels, apparent success at the third level may be illusory and/or short-lived. Indeed, except in the most apolitical or politically unambitious authorities, it is difficult to see how honesty openness and trust could really develop (or survive) if there are no effective mechanisms for resolving political/managerial differences.

2
Taking the Job and Getting Started

Job applications and interviews

With very few exceptions, chief executives and would-be chief executives are ambitious individuals, typically with long-term career objectives. In this context, the choice of which jobs to apply for, and whether or not to accept a post if offered it, is crucial. Misjudgements can adversely affect a chief executive's career trajectory, just as good judgements can substantially enhance it. It is therefore of relevance and interest to explore how chief executives make such judgements. In what circumstances do they apply for and accept a post, and in what circumstances do they withdraw an application or decline an offer?

Much depends on the stage which the chief executive's (or aspirant chief executive's) career has reached. It matters whether a potential applicant is seeking his or her first chief executive role, or whether they already hold a chief executive position. Someone seeking to break into the world of chief executives may be more inclined to 'take a chance' than someone who is seeking a second or third such role.

> *I knew very little about the council when I applied. It was just that I'd reached the stage in my career when I felt I was ready for a chief executive's job...*[1]

Established chief executives are less likely to 'take risks' (although there are exceptions – see below). There is a strong sense of a 'career progression' typically starting with a shire district position

(60 per cent of all English authorities, prior to the 2008 reorganisation in the shire counties were shire districts) and then moving on to a city-based shire district, a small unitary, London borough or smaller Metropolitan District Council (MDC), with the ultimate goal of a large city-based unitary or Metropolitan Borough Council (MBC) or a shire county (and sometimes beyond this to a position elsewhere in the public sector at national or regional level). There are of course many individual exceptions to this pattern. One chief executive interviewed moved from a shire county position to a northern MDC because 'she wanted the challenge of managing a deprived Northern authority'. Indeed the motivation of taking a challenging post to provide a real test of managerial ability was apparent in other cases also.

But there are other important influences. It matters whether or not an applicant has been headhunted; whether or not they are already working in an authority where they are seeking to become a chief executive; and if they are not, how much they know about the political and organisational culture of the authority concerned.

The advantage of applying for one's first chief executive job in an authority where you already work is that the political/organisational culture will be well-known, and a judgement can be made about one's ability to work within it (or possibly transform it). Leadership figures – existing and (up to a point) potential – will also be known, resulting in the capacity for similar judgements about compatibilities. Of the 16 chief executives interviewed, three had achieved their first chief executive job in an authority in which they already worked. A further two chief executives returned at a particular stage in their careers to an authority for which they had worked within the previous decade. The advantages were similar: they were moving into a known cultural milieu with familiar political and managerial personnel (though invariably also some changes and therefore 'unknown quantities').

Three of the chief executives interviewed were 'headhunted' via a firm of consultants for posts which they eventually took. In each case the authorities involved had a relatively problematic public profile, involving difficult leaders (and/or dominant parties) poor CPA performance (actual or anticipated) or claims of corruption. In each case the chief executive thought very carefully about applying for the job. In such cases, the use of informal networks to try to form an accurate picture of the political/organisational climate that would be faced, before taking the job, is of particular importance (although it is also important in other circumstances – see below).

How do prospective chief executives decide whether or not they should apply for a post in a particular authority (or take it if offered). In some cases they will have local knowledge which is helpful.

I'd lived in the area for a while and felt I had a fair grasp of its characteristics and potential.

Where this kind of 'prior knowledge' is absent, there are various channels a prospective chief executive can use, particularly if they are established chief executives (as opposed to 'first post' candidates). The SOLACE network can be used to seek personal insights into the particular strengths and weaknesses of a given authority (Audit Commission CPA reports are of course publicly available). Professional networks for candidates currently heading a profession-based department can also be exploited; for example, a planning officer applying for a chief executive post would have the opportunity to check out the authority with the planning officer (and fellow RTPI member) there. Retiring chief executives may also be prepared to give a briefing.

Whatever an aspirant chief executive can do to gain insights into the political culture of the authority concerned should be followed up. Political culture and traditions vary greatly from one authority to another. There is a world of difference between a conflict-ridden politically-unstable authority such as Kingston-upon-Hull and the relatively benign political environment and traditions of Warwickshire CC. It follows that the challenges facing a chief executive in the former are likely to be more demanding than in the latter. Chief executives in authorities like Walsall, Stoke-on-Trent and North Tyneside, however competent, are always going to have a more difficult task than those in authorities like Wigan, Lancashire and Barnsley, unless there are major cultural transformations in any of these councils.

Pam Fox in her perceptive study of member–officer relations for SOLACE Enterprises identifies a range of circumstances in which problems of member conduct in general and leader/chief executive relationships in particular are more likely to arise. They include the following: (Fox 1998, p. 47ff)

- Unstable politics, for example the following situations
    - a minority administration
    - a fragile coalition
    - one party with a very slender majority
    - a party with a large majority but a factionalised party group
    - adversarial inter-party relations
    - political schisms reinforced by territorial differentiation
    - frequent changes in political control
- Changes in political control, especially between parties with very different philosophies.
- Unclear differentiation of roles and responsibilities of members and officers respectively.
- The existence of a 'blame culture' and a tradition of members behaving aggressively to officers.
- Weak political leadership.
- An external or internal crisis.
- A history of problems of member–officer relations.
- A major discontinuity – for example, the departure of a chief executive coinciding with the departure of a leader.
- Differences in personality between chief executive and leader.

A review of the well-publicised breakdowns in relationships, discussed in Chapters 8 and 9 confirms the relevance of this list of circumstances. Anyone applying for a vacant chief executive post in authorities such as Stoke-on-Trent, Kingston-upon-Hull or Bristol should know what they are letting themselves in for!

Of particular importance to applicants is an understanding of the strengths and weaknesses and leadership style of the current leader. Ultimately however, there is invariably an element of uncertainty which remains.

> Yes I'd checked out the authority. I talked to everyone I knew who had any knowledge of it. So I knew what I was walking into. But there are limits to what you can find out – some of the challenges were ones I hadn't anticipated.

The interview process does provide a final (though by no means easy) opportunity to 'opt-out' if what is picked up about the authority at that stage is not to the liking of the applicant. One chief executive interviewed very nearly did so.

> *I was very critical of the interview process, and nearly didn't take the job as a result. It was all decided on a one hour interview with a limited opportunity for me to ask questions. I thought the council was arrogant to think it could make an informed decision on this basis.*

The interview provides other important opportunities to establish the de facto brief under which the chief executive will operate. In particular, there is the opportunity for the applicant to specify what qualities or priorities he or she will bring to the role (if you appoint me, this is 'what you'll get'). Equally important is the opportunity for the applicant to clarify what is expected of them.

The scope for applicants seeking to clarify what they have to offer can be illustrated by the following examples.

> *I decided to be absolutely upfront at the interview. I told them I could offer integrity, good professional advice and experience of improving performance. I said that they probably wouldn't like some of the advice I'd provide, but that they would know they were getting frank and honest – 'telling it like it is'.*

> *At the interview, I made it clear what my own values were, in particular my enthusiasm for community engagement.... I didn't set out what I would do if appointed – that would have been too pushy – but I did want to give members some sense of what kind of a person they would be appointing.*

The opportunity to discuss the authority's expectations can be similarly illustrated.

> *The members identified two priorities for me – improving the authority's capacity for self-publicity and improving its performance management system. I suggested a third – improving project management.*

> *It was clear from my interview that I would be expected to 'turn things round' in what was a failing authority ... although there was no clear idea from members about what might be involved in doing so.*

It was clear at the interview at the interview that the leader wanted me to work with him to restore the reputation of the authority.

The propensity to be explicit about what an applicant's own priorities would be, if appointed, is greater for established chief executives than for first-time applicants, who are more likely to be wary about appearing too pushy. In several cases a dialogue developed – 'here's what I can offer... what would you expect of me? ... is there a congruence between the two agendas?'

One established chief executive who had been headhunted for a high profile but potentially difficult post went so far as to specify certain conditions which would have to be agreed if he were to take the job – in particular, that after the next election (due in 6 months time) the dominant group, if re-elected, would 'withdraw from micromanagement'. Clearly the specification of conditions is only possible in circumstances where the applicant has a high status and reputation and whose career progression does not depend on taking the job (i.e. is in a strong bargaining position).

There is a further piece of information which some (although by no means all) chief executives had sought before taking the job – 'is there all-party support for my appointment?' This concern is a sensible precaution in authorities where political control is vulnerable to change in the short-medium term. A chief executive appointed without the support of an opposition group which could gain power 6 months later would understandably be apprehensive about his or her standing with the new administration, if this scenario developed.

The period of grace

Several chief executives interviewed made reference to a 'honeymoon period' or 'period of grace' immediately following their appointment. What appeared to be involved was a period of between 6 and 9 months where the newly appointed chief executive was not expected to 'deliver' (on whatever criteria were expected of him or her) but where it was accepted that they would need time to brief themselves about the strengths and weaknesses of the council's managerial structures and personnel, and, equally important, the way in which the political/managerial interface operated.

This opportunity was widely used by the chief executives interviewed, but in different ways. Some did indeed take advantage of this relatively relaxed environment to clarify their own agendas. Typically this learning process was focused on questions such as 'What do the leading politicians expect of me?' 'What are the key external challenges facing the authority?' 'How well-equipped is the current officer structure to deal with them?' 'How clear is the political/managerial division of labour and is it acceptable?' Indications of the answers to these questions are likely to have been sensed during the interview process (and the preparation for it). But the picture will certainly need filling out. Other chief executives have set in motion structural reorganisations at a relatively early stage in their tenure. None of those interviewed had done so, and none felt it would be appropriate, although there were instances of views being developed about the competence (or otherwise) of managerial colleagues within the honeymoon period.

As well as an opportunity for learning, the honeymoon period is also an opportunity for radical action. Members have 'invested' in a new chief executive and will tend to have high expectations of him or her (notwithstanding the 'period of grace'). Thus if a newly appointed chief executive quickly senses that certain issues need to be dealt with urgently, there will be a predisposition to follow his or her advice. One chief executive was clear that this opportunity for radical change was not one to be missed.

> *I got away with things then that I don't think I could now. In particular.... I devised new approaches for consulting the public over council priorities... and ways of opening up the dominant (Conservative) group to enable a more inclusive discussion of their priorities... neither of these initiatives were particularly welcome to the group... but they went along with them....*

Of particular help to the chief executive was the fact that 2 weeks after his appointment, there was a CPA inspection (following a 'difficult' peer group review) in which major weaknesses in the council's operations became apparent. When the critical CPA report was published, the chief executive was able to link his proposals for change to weaknesses identified in the report. There have been several other instances identified of chief executives using CPA reports as a stimulus to change, although rarely at so early a stage in their period of office.

A second chief executive saw a similar opportunity for radical change.

> *The council was in a mess. There was no political vision...the culture-particularly in relation to member officer relations – was truly awful. Members found officers 'unhelpful and unresponsive'; officers thought members were 'unreasonable'...the officer structure was silo-dominated...the majority Labour group was fragmented three ways...the authority was performing badly and a CPA inspection was shortly to take place...*

A nightmare scenario indeed! In this kind of situation, the case for operating a relatively relaxed, exploratory approach for 6–9 months is overridden by the need for urgent and decisive action, which was indeed taken by the chief executive concerned.

> *I set up workshops in informal surroundings to try to establish 'a better relationship' between members and officers.... I managed to convince them that there were shared objectives to deliver good services for local people...they had more in common than they thought! Once this 'common ground' had been recognised...it became more feasible to work out ways of delivering this outcome.*

The point to emphasise is that this operation was an extremely fraught enterprise, given the existing climate of member–officer relations. It would have been much more difficult for a chief executive who had been there for some time (and was probably 'part of the problem') to act in this way. As a newcomer, the chief executive was able to exploit the 'period of grace' and the urgency of the situation to change the culture of the authority in a radical way.

In authorities in which the newly appointed chief executive faces a less urgent agenda, or sees less need for radical action, there remains important opportunities to establish their position. One interviewee saw the opportunities inherent in the 'period of grace' in this way.

> *the first 6–9 months is crucial for a chief executive...if in that period they can establish a credibility – particularly as 'someone the leader can*

work with' and 'someone the staff sees in positive terms' – then they are well set-up for the future.

In other words the lack of immediate pressure to deliver is nevertheless an opportunity to establish a way of working – with political leaders and staff – which will facilitate the 'capacity to deliver' in the future.

Establishing credibility as 'someone the leader can work with' is a major concern for all newly appointed chief executives. In pursuing this aim, there is an important tactical choice. Does the chief executive seek to establish explicit 'rules of engagement' – around differentiation of tasks, appropriate behaviour, relations with the opposition and so on – at a relatively early stage, or is it better to let these understandings develop over time? In making a judgement, chief executives have to quickly develop skills of 'reading the leader' (see Chapter 4). Chief executives have to judge whether a leader would welcome an early opportunity to establish the ground rules, or whether they would feel uneasy about doing so, or regard the request as premature. The choice also depends on whether the chief executive perceives a real problem in this area, in which case there is a particular reason to clarify guidelines, or whether it is seen as unproblematical, in which case the more gradual development of mutual understandings may be appropriate.

The 'wait and see' tactic is illustrated by the following examples.

> I didn't attempt to discuss the ground rules of the relationship... because I sensed the leader would not be happy with that kind of approach. We developed appropriate ways of working as we went along.

> At the interview I felt positive about the leader and felt I could work with him.... I didn't initiate an early discussion about our respective roles and responsibilities... partly because I felt too inexperienced at the time, and partly because I sensed it wasn't necessary.

Other newly appointed chief executives saw it as more important to seek to establish a 'modus operandi' at an early stage.

> I asked the leader what his key priorities were – it became apparent he didn't have any. There was no sense that he was 'in control' of his group.

When the group led by this leader lost power at the next election, the chief executive found it easier to establish a 'way or working' with the leader who replaced him.

> *We needed to discuss how we were going to work together... what principles we should adopt to make the relationship work.*

It was a very productive meeting, which developed a good understanding of the 'rules of engagement' at a relatively early stage in the relationship.

The case for an early discussion also depends on the relative experience of leader and chief executive respectively. 'First-time' chief executives are unlikely to push hard for a clarification of rules, partly because at that stage in their career, they will have little basis for setting an agenda. New leaders may, like new chief executives, need more time to develop views on the topic. How and when an explicit discussion is initiated and by whom is very much a matter of judgement. More experienced chief executives, particularly if they have experienced problems of establishing understandings elsewhere, may be more proactive, particularly if faced with an experienced leader who is likely to have clear ideas about the nature of the relationship. A particular concern for several chief executives interviewed was the need to establish at an early stage their right to brief opposition parties and to clarify the nature and content of such briefing (see Chapter 4).

Once the newly appointed chief executive has reached the point where he or she feels they understand the key challenges facing the authority, which may include issues such as a limited (or absent) strategy, a distaste for partnership working, a participative vacuum, a divided management team, a problematical political culture, or the likelihood of a poor result in an impending CPA inspection, a judgement has to be made about priorities. Are the challenges tackled simultaneously or sequentially? The latter approach is more common.

> *I saw the priority as clarifying some basic values and changing the culture of the authority – particularly member-officer relations... once that had been dealt with, I turned to the job of agreeing strategic priorities.*

> *I quickly identified partnership working as a key problem area...the leading politicians didn't like partnerships; they saw them as an unwelcome alternative to direct responsibility.*

The 'period of grace' though common cannot be guaranteed and is time-limited. One chief executive suffered a crisis of confidence after being in post for 9 months.

> *I'd warned members that things would get worse before they got better...but after nine months it was clear things weren't getting better, and members were beginning to express concerns. I began to wonder whether I was up to the job.*

Fortunately for this chief executive's confidence, improvements began to become apparent soon afterwards.

Problems may also develop for a newly appointed chief executive faced with a leader to whom he or she finds it difficult to relate. One chief executive made a crucial distinction between what he would have done and the problems faced by his successor.

> *What the leader was proposing was basically bad for the town's development prospects. If I'd still been in post, I'd have tried to convince the leader of this and probably resigned if I hadn't been able to...my successor now realises she should have stood up to him, but as a new appointment, with no previous chief executive experience, she found this very difficult...*

The dilemma raises the interesting issues of in what circumstances a chief executive should stand up to a leader not because what the leader wants can't be done, but because the chief executive sees it as 'bad for the area' (see Chapter 6).

There are other instances where real problems can develop at an early stage. One chief executive who thought he had established an understanding with the leader, at the interview, about the need for the Labour group to retract from 'micromanagement', found that after a 'false dawn', during the run-up to local elections, the Labour group having increased its majority, soon 'reverted to type'.

> *They were in the building constantly...and what was most disturbing was the aggressive behaviour of the leader and others to senior officers*

and indeed some junior ones...this was intolerable as far as I was concerned.

This apparent breakdown of what the chief executive thought had been agreed marked the abrupt end of the honeymoon period, and subsequently persisted over a long period, proving a constant problem for the chief executive.

More typically, though, chief executives emerge from the period of grace with their credibility reasonably well-established and with a good understanding of what is expected of them, the political culture of the authority, the informal 'rules of the game' within which they have to operate and the strengths and weaknesses of the management structure and personnel they have inherited. This knowledge provides the basis of the development of a much clearer sense of their own strategic agenda.

3
The Chief Executive as 'Head of Paid Service'

Of all the different 'balancing acts' which chief executives need to perform, probably the most challenging is that between their role as the main conduit with the political side of the council (and in particular with the leadership of the party or parties forming the administration) and their role as the head of paid service.[1] This latter role gives the chief executive the authority in principle to develop an organisational culture which he or she feels can deliver the strategic agenda of the authority (including the political priorities which this is likely to reflect). It also implies an opportunity to build a management team which the chief executive feels he or she can work with to develop the appropriate organisational culture and deliver the strategic priorities. This opportunity implies in turn a degree of influence on appointments and (just as important) on exit strategies for existing management team members who the chief executive feels are unlikely to be supportive of or competent to deliver these goals.

The problem for chief executives is that they are unlikely to be given delegated authority to make the changes they see as being desirable. Leading politicians will often have their own views about the competence of management team members, which may differ from the chief executive's views. They will certainly want to retain responsibility for senior appointments, where they may choose not to take the chief executive's advice. And traditional well-established patterns of political behaviour may be obstructive to the kind of organisational culture the chief executive is seeking to develop – for example, a tradition of members seeking to influence middle managers about ward issues, by contacting them directly.

Changing the culture

How do chief executives deal with this challenge of persuading members to support the changes in culture and personnel which they see as necessary? One of the advantages of the 'period of grace' (see Chapter 3) is that it provides the opportunity for the newly appointed chief executive to carry out some diagnostic work. Is the management team that has been inherited united or divided? Does it tend to operate with a 'silo mentality' or is it capable of joined-up working? What are the strengths and weaknesses of individual management team members? Are there any who need to be 'eased out'? Are there any unsuccessful recent applicants for the chief executive's job who may present particular difficulties? Part of the diagnostic operation is also likely to involve an attempt to assess the organisational culture beyond the management team. In particular are there any indications of major problems – a culture of fear? A lack of enterprise? Are there ways in which the political culture impacts upon the organisational culture (e.g., a degree of contempt for politicians, or -particularly worrying, – evidence of 'special (but informal) relationships' between middle managers and key councillors)? Some chief executives have made a series of forays into the depths of the organisation at an early stage, to try to assess the culture

> I set myself a 'crash induction course'... talking to a wide range of front-line staff, on the basis that you get a more realistic view about organisational strengths and weaknesses from people at this level.

Several chief executives interviewed made significant discoveries during the 'period of grace', which contributed to an agenda for action.

> I soon discovered to my surprise that there was a widespread mistrust of officers on the part of councillors... the view seemed to be that 'the officers have been the opposition here'.... I would present papers outlining proposals for new structures and processes and I'd be quizzed about the detail in a mistrustful and often hostile way... it really opened my eyes to the culture of the place...

> One of my first challenges was to change the very traditional structures and culture of the county. There were 16 departments... much of the

policy making was fragmented; the main driving force was the set of committee chair/chief officer pairings...

I soon realised that there was a 'ruling mafia' in Labour politics in the city... which worked with a wider set of allies, some of them in key positions in city council. One director had a direct line to the leader... so I couldn't even trust my own management team.

I realised that I had inherited an officer-dominated authority. The previous chief executive had seen her role as 'de facto' leader and once famously commented 'members know their place in this authority'... I had to explain to management board that this attitude to politicians had to change...

In essence several of these discoveries involved a recognition on the part of the chief executive of the profound influence of the recent organisational history of the authority, which could not have been picked up (except at a superficial level) during the appointments procedure.

The development of a management action agenda on the chief executive's part is likely to raise a number of issues about the extent to which leading politicians should be involved in 'management' issues, and which will have to be negotiated.

In particular:

- If a chief executive wants to replace particular members of his or her management team, will the political leadership support this process?
- If a chief executive wants to retain particular members of the team that leading politicians think should be replaced, how is this difference of view resolved?
- What should be the respective roles of chief executive and leading members in the appointments procedures of chief officers?
- How are political practices which are detrimental to good management to be dealt with?

Building your own management team

All chief executives would want, as far as possible, to work with a management team of compatible individuals who share the same commitment to the chief executive's own priorities, and who are able to work together to achieve these priorities. Yet, on appointment, chief executives inherit a management team, none of whom they have played a part in selecting. To some extent, the challenge of developing an inherited management team into a coherent unit can be dealt with by 'team building', and many chief executives have indeed initiated such programmes of development. But even given this opportunity, it is by no means uncommon for newly appointed chief executives, after an initial period of 'informal assessment', to conclude that there are one or more management team members with whom they do not think it is likely that they can develop a good (or even adequate) working relationship. In these circumstances, what are the chief executive's options?

The first major type of 'problem colleague' is the disappointed applicant who was not selected to the post filled by the new chief executive.

> *In the run-up to my appointment, the chief executive's job had been 'promised' to the Director of Education ... a 'games-player' to whom I subsequently developed a great dislike. However the appointments panel were persuaded that the job should go to me, against the wishes of the majority group whip ... which caused resentment on the whip's part, and real problems for me with the unsuccessful applicant, who remained a member of the management team ...*

Given the support enjoyed by the Director of Education within the majority group, it was fortunate for the chief executive that there was shortly afterwards a damning OFSTED report on the authority's secondary schools, which meant that the Director's position was no longer tenable and he resigned. This chief executive enjoyed further good fortune when a £2 million overspend and a critical external report meant the Director of Adult Services could also be 'strongly encouraged' to go (and did). The decision of an acting Chief Finance Officer not to apply for a newly created Director of Finance post removed the final obstacle to the chief executive's attempts to bring together a compatible management team (although tensions with this disgruntled chief whip and one or two other leading councillors remained).

An alternative approach to a similar problem was adopted by a second chief executive, who was appointed when the favourite for the job had been the County Treasurer. Her response, knowing that the person concerned was professionally competent, was to use her 'soft skills' (developed during her time as Chief Personnel Officer) to overcome the disaffection of the disappointed candidate which resulted (after a time) in his becoming a co-operative management team member.

Another chief executive realised during the first 2 months of her appointment to a failing authority that most senior officers would have to be replaced. Her attempts to do so met resistance from leading councillors.

Most of the senior managers had been around for 25 years or more, and were much liked by the more experienced councillors...but in my view they were poor managers. I had to deal with several objections from members along the lines of 'but why do we need to get rid of him...

She was successful in overcoming this resistance, and her judgement was vindicated when at the next CPA inspection the authority was reclassified from 'poor' to 'good'.

It is never an easy matter to terminate the employment of a chief officer who is resistant to the idea of leaving. It is that much more difficult to do so without political support, Another chief executive appointed to save a failing authority used the sense of urgency surrounding her appointment to gain political support for her perception that a couple of directors needed to go.

The converse of the problem of easing out un-co-operative or inadequate management team colleagues is dealing with pressure from politicians to get rid of officers they feel to be inadequate.

Soon after my appointment, the Labour leadership told me that they wanted to get rid of the Director of Finance, who they thought was 'unhelpful' – indeed 'over-critical'....However by then I'd formed a positive view of her, I managed to persuade the Labour leadership to give her a chance – they agreed to a six month probation period...

The Director of Finance must have managed to convince the Labour group of her worth because no further attempt was made to dispense with her services.

A similar problem faced a chief executive whose leader demanded that a director who had been subject to external criticism should be sacked. The chief executive did not think that this was appropriate; she regarded the director as 'part of the solution' not the problem'. In her own terms she 'dug her heels in' and saw this, in retrospect, as a situation in which she was right to have stood by her principles.

Another chief executive experienced a more general problem of a leader who had come to the conclusion that he 'didn't rate' or 'couldn't work with' several chief officers whom the chief executive regarded as perfectly competent. She too used her HR skills to persuade the leader to rethink his position.

A further (more unusual) variant of would-be political involvement in who should be in the management team emerged from a 2005 JRF interview.

> The leader, having discovered that he could work with the Head of Economic Development, demanded that this individual should attend management team meetings on a regular basis, I told him I wasn't prepared to accept this...

Even when a recently appointed chief executive has managed to remould the management team to his or her satisfaction, there is the longer-term issue of what role to play in new appointments, when existing (valued) management team colleagues move elsewhere or retire. Clearly, in order to retain a team of compatible chief officers, chief executives would want (at the very least) to have their views taken seriously in any appointments procedure.[2] By and large this outcome was achieved, with only one or two exceptions, including this one, from an earlier (JRF political leadership research) interview.

> The leader and I were reviewing the performances of applicants for a directors job. We agreed that one candidate was outstanding... but when we went back into the sub-committee, an influential colleague expressed a preference for another candidate, and the leader went along with that, despite my protests.

It is much more usual for chief executives to be able to influence appointments in a way which avoids having unwanted candidates foisted on them. At the very least they will end up with a colleague whom they find acceptable (often their 'first preference'). The following experience is typical.

> My view about officer appointments are always given due weight. In 14 years as chief executive, I've never had a director I did not 'want imposed on me.

Dealing with unacceptable political interference

The final area in which a chief executive's role as head of paid service provides a test for the relationship with the leader is the tendency, in some authorities, for politicians to behave in ways which either adversely affects the morale of employees or restricts the chief executive's 'capacity to manage' effectively (or both). Typically what is involved is a transgression of the informal rule that 'members make policy, officers implement it'. As will be discussed in Chapter 10, this informal rule does not equate with reality in many authorities, and this situation is not necessarily problematical, so long as there is a clear understanding as to the ways in which members can reasonably become involved in the detail of implementation or management. It is where member behaviour ignores or challenges such understandings that a chief executive may feel compelled to raise objections – typically through the leader.

There may of course be problems of this nature for chief executives in their personal relationship with the leader. These problems are considered in the next chapter (Chapter 4). The concerns in this chapter are the situations in which a chief executive feels it necessary to act on behalf of the paid service (or particular elements of it) for which he or she is responsible.

Chief executives who had experienced problems of this nature are often fiercely protective of their management team colleagues. One chief executive, faced with a disenchanted and unpredictable opposition leader (formerly council leader), tried to ensure that the brunt of the (often vitriolic) criticisms from this individual were directed at her, and not at other directors. A chief executive in the 2005 JRF political leadership study experienced, and made a major issue of a similar problem.

> I was present at a meeting where the leader gave a public dressing down to one of the directors, who left the meeting with his hands shaking and in tears. After the meeting I asked to meet the leader in private, and told him that I found such behaviour unacceptable and was not prepared to work in an authority in which it took place. I could sense from the leader's body language that he was losing his cool and I expected, when I finished, an explosion! But no; first the leader told me 'never to speak to him like that again' and then said he accepted the basis of my criticism. That was a defining moment.

Change of political control is in many ways a potential hazard for a chief executive, not least if the new leader has formed a critical view of senior staff and chooses to express it at an early stage.

> *The new leader called all the top and second tier officers together and expressed his dissatisfaction with their performance, adding that 'I wouldn't expect more than one third of you to be around in a year's time...' it was hugely damaging to staff morale.*

Again the chief executive concerned saw this outburst as a challenge; an opportunity to apply her human relations skills. She worked hard at developing a way of working with the leader which would change his view (both of the qualities of staff and of what was 'acceptable behaviour') and resisted the pressure from the leader to get rid of some of the management team, arguing that they should at least be given a chance to show that they could deliver the new administration's programme (which they subsequently did). She reassured management team colleagues that she had full confidence in them. Over time, after a few more problematic incidents, this HR approach proved highly effective.

Other chief executives too were similarly explicit about their use of HR skills to resolve similar problems.

> *One of my key roles is to protect other officers from belligerent political pressure and to resolve difficult issues where politicians appear to be losing confidence in an officer...*

Another chief executive emphasised the need for a 'united front' in this kind of situation.

> The deputy leader was very bright...but tended to lose his temper at the slightest provocation. Sometimes these outbursts would be directed at me, sometimes at other directors...my job was to ensure that there was collective 'spirit' in the management team.... I kept other directors informed, supported them when they were given a hard time and sometimes took up an issue that had been raised with them myself. A united front was essential.

In other cases the problem is not that of a leader (or deputy's) behaviour but with a backbench maverick.

> There is one councillor who has been involved in micro management – in relation to council housing.... I've asked the leader to 'rein him in', which he's agreed to do, although I know he'll find it difficult.

Particularly problematical for a chief executive is the situation where a relatively weak leader (in terms of group discipline) is not prepared to act in this way.

> At the moment too many members are spending too much time listening to staff criticisms about the way the authority is being managed. That's created real difficulties for me.

His experience is symptomatic of a wider problem – a situation where the chief executive does not feel he can trust his or her staff in their dealings with councillors. In addition to the above example, there is the problem of local authorities where either there are 'political placements' or there are officers with a 'direct line' to leading members. The reference to the Labour 'ruling mafia' (see Chapter 9, p. 127) provides an example of the latter. Another chief executive had problems with political placements.

> We've recently introduced a scheme of 'political assistants' – mainly to move away from the 6 or 7 'politicised officers' in this authority who have been used as informal contacts by the political groups. There's a long tradition of this here, which I think this is totally unacceptable.

One of the skills of a good chief executive is that of recognising and exploiting an opportunity to change a problematic pattern of intrusive member behaviour as in the following case.

> *Soon after my appointment, I recognised that the impending move to unitary status was a great opportunity to eliminate the traditional Welsh micro-management practices – housing allocations, staff appointments, that kind of thing.... I was able to persuade the new council to accept 'good practice' arrangements, which did away with previous practice.*

For chief executives who cannot (often through no fault of their own) generate a requisite level of trust amongst the senior officer cadre, or who cannot persuade politicians to change behaviour which undermines management capacity, there is something of an impasse. In these circumstances responding by moving to another job may ultimately be the best solution.

It should be emphasised that this chapter has focused on 'problems' of member behaviour seen from the perspective of chief executives, and that what is viewed as 'inappropriate councillor behaviour' by chief executives may be viewed as entirely appropriate by members, for example the facility for members to contact, and to seek to persuade officers at different levels of the hierarchy. In this respect – as in many others – managerial and political logic may point in different directions.

Although issues of unacceptably intrusive member behaviour could in principle be regulated by a member-officer protocol, there was very little support amongst the chief executives interviewed for this kind of response. Typically, there was a view that a more informed set of 'shared understandings' was preferable. In one authority, the chief executive felt that 'the regular use of the protocol showed that we were failing to establish a good working relationship'. Another chief executive felt that in the difficult political climate of her authority, a protocol would largely be ignored. There was however, more support for a protocol to regulate responses to an authority becoming hung (see Chapter 6). The judgement as to when to argue for formal rules (such as protocols) and when to rely on informal rules (or shared understandings) is one which chief executives have to make in many situations.

4
Managing the Relationship with the Leader

It was noted in Chapter 2 that some chief executives sought to establish clear guidelines covering their relationship with the leader soon after appointment (indeed, occasionally, during the appointment process itself), although at this stage in the relationship, such guidelines typically covered role definitions rather than behavioural issues, plus particular concerns of the chief executive, such as the relationship with the opposition party or parties. Others chose not to raise such issues explicitly, preferring to see how the relationship developed, and to rely on a mutual informal understanding of these guidelines (although occasional explicit negotiation was seen to be required).

Over time, all chief executives will find themselves analysing this most crucial of relationships and seeking to develop a way of working (backed by a set of mutual understandings) which enables them to do a good job as the key strategic manager of the authority. In particular, although the *functional* ('who does what') elements of the relationship can be established fairly quickly (and in some circumstances there will be a strong case for doing so) the *behavioural* framework of the relationship will inevitably take longer to establish, and may never be the subject of an explicit discussion. It will develop gradually as the two individuals experience a range of situations which generate responses (implicit or explicit) from one or both, which contribute to a growing understanding of the behavioural dynamics of the relationship.

In the development of the relationship (from the chief executive's perspective) there is a sequence of issues which will need to be addressed (although in some circumstances they can be dealt with relatively easily). The sequence is as follows:

- What needs to be resolved urgently?
- Gaining an understanding of the political context within which the leader operates (including the extent to which the designated leader is in fact the 'real leader')
- Developing an ability to 'read the leader'.

Once a satisfactory modus operandi has been achieved, it is helpful to explore the relevance of the marriage metaphor, which was used in one way or another by several of the chief executives interviewed. The leader/chief executive relationship is like a marriage... or is it?

What needs to be resolved urgently?

Even for chief executives who are inclined to allow a relationship to develop organically, there may be issues they feel it is imperative to identify and resolve at an early stage. One example is provided by the chief executive who sought an assurance from his leader that the majority group would withdraw from micromanagement (see Chapter 2), an assurance which was not in the event put into practice.

Several chief executives identified their relationship with opposition groups as an issue that required early resolution.

> *Soon after I arrived, I realised that there was a long tradition of the chief executive 'telling the opposition nothing'.... I've always thought that this was unacceptable, and I made it clear that I wanted to brief opposition leaders when I felt it to be appropriate to do so... there was some resistance from the Labour group, but not from the leader, who accepted the principle.*

Other chief executives confirmed that briefing opposition groups was a point of principle for them. Some had experienced resistance, some did not.

> *I insisted on briefing the opposition leader, in the face of reluctance on the part of the coalition leaders... we had disagreements about what the*

> *Conservative leader should and shouldn't be told. I wanted to be trusted to use my judgement.*

Another chief executive explained how he used his judgement in this respect.

> *Briefing of opposition groups should be on the basis that they should never be surprised by something which blows up which is potentially important to the authority, like an impending social services overspend.*

Again it should be recognised that there may sometimes be sound political reasons why a council leader may not wish opposition groups to learn of such problems.

Occasionally, other issues such as press briefings, roles in partnerships (including who takes the chair) or political involvement in an impending CPA visit have been raised by a chief executive at an early stage.

Understanding the political context

Who is the leader?

This may seem a pointless (or rhetorical) question, but it is not always so. In a sense it can be seen as one element in the more general task of understanding and coming to terms with the political culture, but it is a particularly urgent piece of understanding, well illustrated by the situation which was identified by a chief executive in one of our JRF (2005) case studies.

> The hung authority operates on 'six-monthly' terms for leaders – Conservative, Labour and Liberal Democrat leaders alternate... the transition from Councillor X being leader to not being leader can be described as 'seamless' – nobody seemed to notice that he wasn't still the leader... he has more clout than the formal leader because he's in the council offices all the time... whatever the formal position might be. Councillor X is still at the forefront of virtually everything...

Indeed, in this authority the de facto leader also operated up to a point as de facto chief executive, given that the individual who held this post was doing so on an 'acting' basis, never wanted the position in the first place and was not relishing his responsibilities. For a newly appointed chief executive in this authority, the question of 'who is the leader' would have been a very pertinent one.

Another newly appointed chief executive soon discovered that leadership was in effect shared between three key figures – the designated leader, his deputy and the chief whip (a situation reflecting a 'collegiate' view of leadership which finds particular favour with Liberal Democrat executives).

> The leader did not seem to want one-to-one meetings, which I felt were essential ... he always brought along the deputy and the chief whip ... it was she who had opposed my appointment, and I found it really hard to work with her ...

In another case, the chief executive was faced with more of a power imbalance than a shared approach to leadership in a hung authority.

> I soon recognised that the deputy leader (Lib Dem) was a more important figure than the leader (Labour) and that there was little point in one-to-one meetings with the latter. It made sense to see leadership as a dual role and to meet with them on this basis.

There was a further incongruity in this situation when the Labour leader of the council had the whip withdrawn by the Labour group, but continued in formal terms, as council leader. This was an extremely difficult situation for the chief executive concerned. She had to consult the 'leader of the Labour group' on a regular basis, whilst knowing that the 'unattached' council leader would continue to represent the council in partnership working. Fortuitously, the situation was resolved by the result of an election three months later.

Indeed one interviewee was placed in a situation whereby there was no leader – or leadership group – to deal with, and he became 'de facto' council leader.

> Three months before the 2002 election the Liberal Democrats passed a vote of no confidence on the Conservative minority administration and called on them to resign, arguing in public that the chief executive could

run the authority without a political executive, in the interim. The next week I was on the front page of the MJ.

The chief executive concerned accepted it (he may not have had a lot of choice) as part of the pre-election freneticism which he knew would be resolved in May (which indeed it was).

Relationship between the leader and the group

These illustrations demonstrate that the question 'who is the leader?' is not always an academic one. A more common problem for chief executives is a situation where there is a recognised leader, but one with a somewhat tenuous relationship with his or her group which means that the leader's ability to speak for the group cannot always be relied upon. If this is the case, it is a crucial insight for chief executives in developing an understanding of the political context, with a range of problematical implications.

> *The problem lies in the leader's relationship with the group... it is not a factionalised group, but there are some strong individuals in it... the leader does not consult as much as he should; he has ideas and expresses them to me, but I can't be sure whether they will be acceptable to the executive, or the group.*

The chief executive realised that she had to use other channels (the deputy leader, and other key figures) to check things out, which she acknowledged was a potential threat to the quality of her relationship with the leader, although it hadn't yet surfaced.

Another chief executive was aware that the leader, on whose ability to 'speak for the group' he used to be able to rely, was now less able to do so, as the Conservative group had expanded in size and now included a number of individuals less inclined to follow a lead from the leader.

> *The leader has always been enthusiastic about the Pathfinder scheme (covering two-tier working arrangements). The problem is there is a wave of opinion within the Conservative group which evaluates joint working in terms of 'what's in it for our authority'? The leader seems less able to influence the group over this issue than she was in 2006.*

In an example from the JRF (2005) study, a chief executive witnessed first-hand evidence of a leader's dependence on other colleagues.

> In reality, the leader was heavily dependent on the views of his deputy... you could see him at cabinet meetings checking out her body language... if she shook her head, you knew he wouldn't pursue it... his skill was to sense the momentum of the meeting and then 'front' it.

A further problem chief executives sometimes have to face is a factionalised majority group in which the leader is constantly under pressure from different factions. In one case a deposed leader presented a particular problem – for the chief executive as much as the current leader.

> *The previous leader did everything she could to undermine him, to enhance her chances of re-election... every opportunity was taken to make life difficult for him (and me), so much so that his health deteriorated and he had to stand down...*

The challenge for the chief executive is to figure out as soon as possible the relationships between the leader and the group he or she represents, and between the leader and the cabinet which he or she heads. In a majority-control situation, the two issues are likely to be similar: if a leader is 'in control' of the group, he or she is likely to be in control of the cabinet also. On the other hand if he or she cannot speak for the cabinet, they are unlikely to be able to speak for the party group. In a hung situation, there may be more variation: a leader may have the full confidence of his or her group, but struggle to persuade a coalition-based cabinet. Working with a leader who can 'deliver', which was the situation enjoyed by the majority of the chief executives interviewed, is a much more straightforward situation than one where there is a leader who cannot do so (whether for reasons of group factionalism or limited personal skills).

Reading the leader

Several chief executives used the term 'reading the leader' to describe what they saw as an essential ingredient in the development of an effective relationship. In fact no chief executive/leader relationship starts with a totally blank sheet of paper. If the chief executive is an internal appointee (or someone 'returning' to a previous base) then there is likely to have been some kind of history of previous interaction, through which both leader and chief executive will have formed an impression of the other (this 'previous knowledge' is also important when there is change of political control, or indeed of leadership within a majority party – see Chapter 5).

One internally promoted chief executive first had dealings with his leader when he (the chief executive) was a senior personnel officer and the leader was chair of the Personnel Committee (pre-2000 Act).

> *It was helpful that the leader was himself a personnel officer in another authority, at the time. He gave me a tough time at first, but we soon developed a good relationship, partly because we 'spoke the same language'.*

A second chief executive recognised advantages in the fact that the leader was a retired academic.

> *...there are things we can discuss and resolve on equal terms...for example we drew Venn diagrams together to clarify the way our roles and responsibilities should be sorted out...*

In another case, advantage was seen in the fact that the chief executive and leader had both been brought up in the same South London suburb.

> You can't manufacture these things, but you can make the most of them when they happen.

In most circumstances, however the new chief executive and the leader will have little to go on, beyond impressions formed during the interview process (and, in the case of the chief executive, any pre-interview research carried out). The value of 'prior research' is illustrated by the experience of a chief executive moving from a shire county to a northern MBC, who was well aware of the strength of the 'double act', half of which she was replacing ('who am I replacing? is often a pertinent issue which merits careful thought).

> *I had very good reports of the leader...which were totally justified...however there was a problem of following the renowned 'double act'...the leader wanted our relationship to be similar, whereas I soon decided I wanted it to be different.*

The importance of developing a swift understanding of the relationship between the leader and his or her cabinet/group has already been discussed. There is a further important element of political understanding for the chief executive. 'Where is the leader coming from?' is the way it was often expressed. The essence of this concern is to understand the career trajectory of the leader. Is he or she working towards a parliamentary candidature? Or a senior role in the Local Government Association? Or is it a case of enjoying an unexpected tenure of office before retirement? These things matter; a prospective parliamentary candidate will be much more likely to follow his or her national party's line – indeed to embrace it enthusiastically where this is seen to be advantageous. There will be more concern about the way the performance of the authority is assessed (this concern also applies to those who seek high office in the Local Government Association (LGA)). One's credibility is enhanced by an excellent CPA rating. An understanding of the career aspirations of a leader enables chief executives 'to put yourself in his/her place' and predict/understand why, for example, a county Conservative leader might not choose to pursue a bid for unitary status in the 2006–2008 reorganisation process.

'Reading the leader' is just as important in the behavioural sense as it is in the political sense ('knowing where the leader is coming from'); indeed often more so. From the various responses provided in the interviews, it is possible to set out a check list of key features in the pursuit of this objective.

- Dealing with 'big ideas'
- Dealing with a leader's limited attention span
- Dealing with a leader's volatile temperament.

Big ideas

There are two issues here. How does a chief executive respond to leaders (of whom there are several) who tend to come up with 'big ideas' and expect if not an immediate response, a relatively quick one? Conversely, in what circumstances do chief executives introduce ideas which they want the leader to take seriously? In relation to the first question, one chief executive felt that his role was to act as a 'sieve' for the stream of the leader's big ideas.

> He'd regularly come up with things he felt we should do... like 'they've got this new waste incinerator in Woking; we should have one...'. I'd respond by saying something like 'great idea, leader, but let's have a look at the feasibility and costs before we move on it...'. I felt I had to be supportive – indeed enthusiastic – but at the same time realistic.

In another case:

> The leader is an 'ideas man'... he often throws them into the conversation, but he will listen to me in relation to their feasibility, and on the way they should be implemented. I try to be as helpful as possible, but sometimes you do have to draw attention to the problems.

A chief executive in 2005 JRF political leadership research operated a less diplomatic way (which was however appropriate in terms of the dynamics of the relationship he had developed with the leader).

> The leader marched into my office with the owner of the local theatre and said 'we're going to buy the theatre for £2 million'. I replied 'no we're not'... after a lot of discussion we reached a resolution. If he could organise the sale of the redundant Market Hall, then we'd follow up the theatre option.

In general chief executives preferred leaders who were proactive in policy terms to those who were not, but felt that they had responsibility to ensure that random big ideas were compatible with the council's corporate strategy (or could be 'repackaged' to become so).

Chief executives will also often wish to try out ideas on leaders and will need to make judgements about the circumstances in which leaders are likely to be most responsive.

> The leader prefers 'big ideas' to be dropped into conversations casually...this gives him time to consider them without feeling pressured...and we can then return to them after a suitable interval.

Another chief executive quickly recognised the value of the many car journeys he shared with the leader, going to meetings in a large county, as a mechanism for introducing such ideas.

> Most of the 'real business' is done informally on car journeys...the weekly meeting at County Hall is a more formal affair, where it would be more difficult to have the kind of exploratory discussions we would need to have about new ideas.

One of the key elements of a good relationship (see Chapter 7) is the 'no surprises' principle. Informal settings often provide the best mechanism for a chief executive to apply this principle, particularly if the surprise is an unwelcome one.

When to introduce a 'big idea' is a specific illustration of a more general problem of managing a conversation with a leader to ensure a productive outcome (in the chief executive's terms).

> The leader does sometimes dig his heels in. I can read the signs that he is becoming increasingly obdurate...in which case I withdraw, and reconsider the issue, and try to find a way of responding positively, but in terms I feel comfortable with.

> I know when the leader is getting angry about something – his demeanour, his body language changes – and I realise I have to drop the issue and find another way of introducing it.

> You don't raise a difficult issue with a leader when he's tired or in a bad mood.

Conversely, chief executives sometimes find their own body language picked up by a perceptive leader, in which case it can provide an opportunity for a productive discussion.

> The new leader had obviously watched me closely at a partnership meeting and said afterwards, 'you weren't happy with that, were you?'

Dealing with a short attention span

A second challenge facing some chief executives is an awareness that the leader has a relatively short attention span.

> *The leader has a very short attention span... as a result. I discontinued the programmed weekly meetings... we still meet regularly but not in a structured way, and we talk a lot on the phone...*
>
> *I soon recognised that the leader had a low boredom threshold and that I needed to reach decisions with him as speedily as possible.*

Both these examples illustrate a more general point, namely that chief executives usually feel that they have to adjust their preferred style of working to that of the leader, and not to expect the leader to necessarily make similar adjustments. Hence there are problems in the use of the marriage analogy (see Chapter 4, p. 61 below).

Dealing with a leader's volatile temperament

In general chief executives prefer not to have rows with leaders; to do so implies a breakdown of civilised relations. However, given that some leaders, by temperament, do not share the same reluctance, chief executives sometimes have to find a way of dealing with outbursts of temper. Responses vary (also no doubt influenced by temperament).

> *You can have rows with some leaders, if that's part of the way they operate, but not with others.*
>
> *You shouldn't lose your cool too often... not least because if you do it rarely, it's taken seriously by the leader.*

There is a particular problem for chief executives if a leader's outbursts of temper take place in a public arena with partner representatives present.

> *His outbursts were particularly problematical for me in partnership meetings, where I've tried to establish the basis for a good working relationship... only for the leader to ruin it.*

And it's even worse if the anger is personally directed at a chief executive in such arenas. The following example relates to a former leader;

had it been an existing leader it is difficult to see how the chief executive could have continued in post.

> At a meeting of leaders in the city region, our leader put forward an agreed council position... the former leader challenged it.... I then confirmed that it had been agreed, whereupon she pointed at me and called me a liar...

Sometimes a loss of temper on the part of a leader is a reflection of a crisis or critical incident (see Chapter 8) and heightens the pressure for its resolution.

At their worst temper outbursts are part of a 'bullying' behaviour syndrome. One chief executive described her first chief executive appointment in the following terms.

> It was a baptism of fire... the leader was an experienced politician who used to regularly shout and rant at me... if I'd been a man he might well have hit me.... I deliberately chose to use the fact that I was a woman to try to deal with his behaviour...

Fortunately for the chief executive concerned, the leader was ousted by his party group within a year of her appointment, and the new leader was inexperienced, more equable, and more prepared to respond to her advice.

For a chief executive to be faced with this kind of behaviour is rare. It does illustrate the limits to the laudable aim of 'reading the leader' and then using that knowledge to develop a positive and mutually acceptable way of working. In most cases, however, the philosophy of one chief executive (which was shared by many respondents) has proved to be effective.

> You have to be able to 'put yourself in the place' of the leader... to be able to get 'inside their mind' if you like. You can do this by listening carefully to what they say... even if they are not explicit about their assumptions and priorities, you can deduce them... you can then present advice and options to them in a way which is compatible with their assumptive world.

In developing and strengthening the relationship, there are various things which chief executives can do (depending on the circumstances). They can support a new and inexperienced leader faced with aggressive opposition (sometimes within the leader's party rather than the political opposition).

> *I put in a lot of effort with the new leader, supporting and encouraging him, and feeding him with information to support arguments he wanted to make against the deposed leader...*

They can seek to stiffen a leader's resolve, when under challenge from within his or her party group, or from public opinion.

> *We had a policy for closing failing schools in the county... in one particular case there was a public outcry, and the leader began to waver and think about reversing the decision.... I managed to persuade him that it would undermine the whole policy if he did so...*

The need to 'keep talking', to 'avoid complacency', to 'keep the leader informed' were all emphasised. 'Keeping the leader informed' did not just apply to important external pressures or internal problems which would necessitate difficult decisions in the short-term (e.g. the likelihood of a poor CPA result, or an impending social services overspend). It could be extended to the provision of information about differences of opinion within the management team (e.g. the likely strong resistance of a director to a proposed budget cut), often as a quid-pro-quo for similar information about the dynamics of the executive and the majority group.

> *Our discussions often included the leader's problems with his group, and mine with my management team... which really helped us both understand the context within which the other worked.*

All these initiatives can be seen as examples of things chief executives can do to help or support leaders (although in each case there were real benefits for the chief executive also). Without implying an explicitly instrumental motive, they can also be seen as contributions to a co-operative working relationship, where a chief executive can actually help a leader operate more effectively in his or her political sphere, and hence, perhaps, become more ready to help a chief executive deal with a managerial agenda. The concept of mutual dependency – sometimes mutually recognised – is an important one in understanding the dynamics of leader/chief executive relationships. So too is the concept of 'negotiated order'. As we have seen leaders and chief executives have different agendas, which will not always be compatible. Ways have to be found of dealing with these incompatibilities. If a 'good' working relationship has developed (see Chapter 7) such challenges are much more likely to be confronted and resolved than if it has not.

The marriage analogy

Can the 'marriage' analogy be sustained on the basis of the discussion set out in their chapter? Most respondents were doubtful. There were some parallels but also some key differences.

A recent SOLACE publication expressed the following view.

> The leader/chief executive is probably the second most important relationship after your marriage, but you don't get to choose your partner. It's business, not personal... the relationship puts more responsibility on you, whereas marriage is more of a shared partnership.
>
> (SOLACE 2008)

That view was supported by all the interviewees with whom the 'marriage' analogy was discussed, except for one particularly forceful individual who thought that it was – or should be – a relationship based on equality. Other respondents emphasised that the onus was on a chief executive to adjust to a leader.

> *You have to accept the personality/style of the leader and adjust your behaviour and style to him or her – you can't reasonably expect him to do the same to you...*

This view doesn't mean that chief executives should not stand up to bullying or aggressive tactics, nor challenge a leader if they feel his or her decision preferences are unjustified (on an evidence or proprietary basis). It does mean however that the 'ways of doing business' necessarily reflect the leader preferred style rather than that of the chief executive. It may be possible to negotiate changes, although if the leader's approach is embedded in a traditional set of assumptions about what 'political leadership' should involve in the authority, rather than a personal preference, this may prove particularly difficult.

5
Dealing with Political Change

Establishing a relationship with a leader who was instrumental in appointing you is one thing. Doing so with a new leader from the same party is likely to involve problems of re-negotiation of the ground rules and adjustment to a different style of political leadership, but it is likely (although by no means certain) to involve a significant element of continuity. The new leader is from the same party that you have worked with previously, whose priorities and programmes are unlikely to change substantially (although there is generally scope for a new leader to make adjustments within the broad ambit of policy and occasionally to introduce major changes in policy direction). The main challenge facing a chief executive which results from political change is when one political party loses power to another, and a chief executive is faced with a new leader who has previously led (or played a leading role in) an opposition party.[1]

In these circumstances the ability on the part of the chief executives to develop a productive relationship is dependent on a number of influences. Had they anticipated the possibility (or probability) of a change in power? Had they prepared for it, and if so, in what way? How did they go about overcoming any unease or mistrust on the part of the new leader?

One of the reasons newly appointed chief executives are often so insistent in seeking the right to brief opposition leaders on a regular basis (and sometimes have to overcome resistance from current council leaders in doing so) is that they recognise the way in which this process may facilitate a (relatively) smooth transition to a new negotiated order, following a change in political control.

One chief executive's experience illustrates the value of this kind of precedent.

> Did the new leader trust me?...yes, because we'd managed to establish open transparent and inclusive procedures some time ago. There was no way in which I was viewed as the Labour group's protégé. The main challenge was to help equip the new leadership to understand what the job involved, and to strengthen their confidence.

Anticipation and preparation for political change

There are some authorities where political change is a regular occurrence. One chief executive interviewed had worked with four different political administrations (and four different leaders) over a period of 8 years. Another had experienced five such changes (mainly between different variants of no overall control over a similar period). The advantage for chief executives in politically fluctuating authorities is that 'briefing the opposition' is less likely to be perceived as a problem, because everyone knows that 'the opposition' may be in power, or part of a coalition after the next election.

Two of the chief executives interviewed had experienced a succession of leaders from the same party over a relatively short period of time. In the face of this kind of instability, 'anticipation and preparation' may be well-nigh impossible. It is more a case of responding to change as it happens.

In some cases an unexpected change of leader (within the same party) proves extremely welcome. 'First-time' chief executives may be so pleased to be offered the job, that they play down any doubts they may have about the leader, only to discover real problems when they are in post.

> My first leader was useless – he was idealistic, politically naïve and couldn't judge the mood of his group...after a year he was replaced, fortunately for me, by a new leader who had political sensitivity, who knew when he could deliver the group and when he couldn't, and who respected my judgement.

Thus unexpected change can be as positive experience, although other chief executives have struggled with an unanticipated change of leader, as this experience of a chief executive from the 2005 JRF research shows.

> When the new leader was elected, my first task was to confront him with evidence of a potentially fraudulent expenses claim – it was not a promising start... it turned out that he had none of the qualities you normally associate with leadership... he also suffered from a major 'insecurity syndrome'; he was the leader only because there was no other credible candidate.

There was a particularly interesting example of 'preparation for change' from one chief executive. In a hung but Conservative-led council it became clear soon after the 2001 election that the council leader would stand down within a 2-year period. Would-be leaders began to manoeuvre for position. The chief executive was impressed by one of the candidates and worked with him in the run-up to the change in a way which many chief executives would not have contemplated, on the grounds that it would draw them too much into the political sphere (see Chapter 6).

> *I respected his ability and saw his leadership as 'good news' for the authority if he succeeded... whereas his main opponent was much less convincing.... I developed a rapport with him and provided him with advice and briefing, as a help in his bid for the leadership.*

When the chief executive's favoured candidate won the leadership election, there was indeed a good base for a productive working relationship. There might have been problems for the chief executive if he had lost!

Dealing with a change in control

The main potential problem for a chief executive is a switch of power from one party to another, in a situation where there is a tradition of polarised party politics, and a consequent question mark over the readiness of the newly elected party (and leaders) to trust or be able to work with a chief executive who has served their political opponents, often for a considerable period of time. The difficult kind of negotiation that can ensue is illustrated by the following example.

> *A few months before the 2006 election the opposition leader asked for a meeting with me... he started by saying 'I expect to be council leader in three months time, so it's likely I'll be working closely with you.... I start from the premise of not trusting you... can you convince me that I should?*

In fact the chief executive concerned regarded the leader-in-waiting's approach as sensible, and saw it as his job to convince him, which in due course he succeeded in doing.

There are occasions where sheer good luck plays a part in smoothing the transition, although it could be argued in the following case that the luck was deserved.

> *When I was first appointed, Conservatives were in control... at one of the first council meetings I attended, the Labour leader was subjected to virulent public criticism because of a performance failure she had highlighted... she left the council chamber in tears. I made a point of telling her afterwards that I thought the way she'd been treated was totally out of order.*

That message was relayed back to the Labour group, and when they unexpectedly became the largest party, and formed a minority administration, at the next election, they were much more well-disposed to him than they would have been had the incident not taken place.

The value of anticipation (and acting upon that anticipation) was illustrated by the actions of one chief executive.

> *I realised that it was highly likely the Liberal Democrats would cease to be largest party in May 2006... so, on the night of the election, I sought out all four of the party leaders, and made it clear that I would be available from 10.00 the next day to discuss possible options. From these discussions, I formed the view that Labour were interested in running the council, that the other groups weren't and that there were no coalitions possible amongst the three other groups.*

The outcome of the election was that Labour emerged as the largest group. The Labour leader asked to see the chief executive at 11.00 the next morning (no other group contacted her). She took advantage of the two hours prior to this scheduled meeting to summon her management team to prepare for the meeting with the Labour leader, by going through the Labour manifesto and preparing an agenda for the chief executive to take up with the leader. There were three key items.

- What are your priorities – in particular what are the things you want me to deliver over the next year?
- There is some 'unfinished business' left over from the previous administration – can you let us know how you want to deal with it?
- We (chief executive and leader) need to discuss how we are going to work together – what principles we need to agree to make the relationship work?

The subsequent meeting was extremely productive. The chief executive and the leader quickly established a rapport, and dealt with the agenda, even to the extent of establishing some principles of working together. The whole episode represents something of a 'model' case study of a chief executive anticipating political change, acting on the anticipation, and quickly establishing a set of ground rules with the new leader. It was a good piece of opportunity-taking, which, however, relied crucially on the leader playing his part. With other leaders it might not have worked.

In Chapter 3, a further example of a highly mistrustful new leader (following a change in power) was discussed – the leader who called the top tier of managers together and indicated that for two-thirds of them their days were numbered. That new leader presented a challenge for the chief executive, not just in terms of protecting her management team from summary dismissal, but also of developing a manageable one-to-one relationship with the new leader.

> *It soon became apparent that the new leader didn't really trust me...he thought I was too closely associated with the previous Liberal*

> *Democrat/Labour administration ... he never actually used these words, but there were plenty of clues that that was what he felt.*

The first few months were the most difficult of this chief executive's period of office. The leader created huge difficulties for her, not just in relation to his attack on the senior officers. Two weeks after the Conservatives came to power there was an Adult Social Services inspection. The new leader told the inspectors that the service was useless and that it was all the fault of the previous administration and the officers. As a result the authority received a 'no star' rating, which subsequently materially affected its CPA result. He also disregarded the normal 'no surprises' principle on several occasions making statements in public arenas with no prior warning to the chief executive, but with implication for action that were problematic, and (from her perspective) really needed to have been discussed beforehand.

In these circumstances, many chief executives would have quickly scanned the 'job vacancies' columns of the relevant journals. But there are often good reasons not to respond in this way; a move may be very disruptive to family life, particularly the stability of children's education. In this case, the chief executive metaphorically gritted her teeth and set out to establish an acceptable working relationship.

> *I tried to avoid rows.... I never disagreed with the leader in public – that would have been disastrous – but I did tell him firmly afterwards about things he'd done or said that had caused problems for me.... I tried to operate the 'I'm OK; you're OK' principle ... and gradually things did begin to improve.*

The value of an HR background was clear in this case. Chief executives without the skills (and patience) exhibited here would have found it difficult to continue. As it was, the chief executive was able to deliver some changes which were important to the leader in the short-term, which helped her credibility, and there then occurred some timely pieces of 'good news' – for example, a much improved Social Services assessment. After a difficult 12 months, the climate of leader/chief executive interaction (and member/officer relations generally) was described in glowing terms by both participants.

Another chief executive had a similar experience following a change of control.

> At 4.00 am in the morning of the election night in 2002 it became clear that the Conservatives had won. The Conservative leader gave a totally inappropriate speech – not thanking the returning officer or anyone else for that matter – and then pointed at me and said 'Right – in my office at 9.00 am tomorrow'!

The chief executive found this behaviour 'totally inappropriate' but refrained from commenting on it the next morning in the hope that it was a 'one-off'. That proved a good judgement; after a period of skirmishing, a good working relationship developed in which the chief executive found ways of adjusting to the new leader's somewhat abrasive style. It was helpful for her credibility that she had offered regular meetings to the Conservative leader when they were in opposition, even though the offer had not been taken up.

Sometimes anticipation of a change of control may be a factor in motivating a chief executive to apply for jobs elsewhere, particularly if he or she had reached a stage in their career where a change could be justified for other reasons.

> When I decided to apply for the other jobs the then Conservative opposition leader said to me 'I hope you're not going because you think we'll win the next election and that you'd have problems working with us.... I'd be happy to work with you'.

However, the concern of the chief executive was the strong possibility of the election of a different Conservative leader, whom she disliked personally, and with whose policy priorities she disagreed.

> I could have delivered on the policies, but couldn't have coped with my personal antipathy to him.

Dealing with a defeated (or returning) leader

The importance of striving to retain the goodwill of a defeated leader is well illustrated by two of Pam Fox's (Fox 1998, pp. 30ff) case studies. In one case

> the leader had recently regained his position having previously been unseated. He was bitter about his loss of leadership and had

sought to take revenge against those he saw as being responsible. The chief executive had become a particular target for the campaign of revenge. The leader's view is that the chief executive allowed himself to become too closely aligned with the policies of the former administration. He has made attempts to engineer the chief executive's departure by constantly questioning his advice, judgement and actions, communicating with him in a very threatening and abusive manner, attempting to enlist the support of others in undermining him and making derogatory remarks about him outside the authority.

In the second case:

> the problems concern the behaviour of leading members of the opposition group towards staff. The members concerned have failed to come to terms with loss of power, particularly their reduced access to information. Their bitterness is witnessed in their repeated attacks on officers who they see as being too supportive of the ruling alliance's policies. The members' aggressive behaviour... has been particularly directed towards the chief executive, who they accuse of being merely an agent of the ruling alliance. In addition to verbal abuse, they have also adopted tactics such as attempting to exploit any differences of opinion between the chief executive and other officers, trying to undermine his authority by constantly questioning his right to take action on matters...and generally looking for opportunities to embarrass him.

Whilst the second example illustrates the importance of seeking to maintain a good relationship with the leadership group of a deposed administration, there are clearly difficulties if access to information and briefings are requested which a chief executive cannot reasonably provide, within the normal (and necessary) expectations regarding the differential provision of information to administration and opposition respectively. The first example is even more difficult for a chief executive to resolve. It is unreasonable that a deposed leader from a party which continues to form an administration to expect preferential treatment, although it is not unknown for deposed leaders to continue to behave as though they were still in power, and to expect a level of officer support commensurate with this (illusory) status! Equally there is no way a chief executive could provide such support, in the face of his or her need to build a relationship with the new leadership.

What emerged from the interviews was that although political change can be a problem for a chief executive, it need not be. It is understandable that opposition leaders, in authorities with a history of political conflict, may be initially mistrustful of the chief executive, and feel they need to be convinced of his or her capacity to deliver their priorities, which are likely to be very different from those of their predecessors. But there are many chief executives who can set up and make use of lines of communication with opposition leaders, in a way which helps to overcome some of these doubts. As a crucial election approaches, there is a possibility of preparing the ground for an outcome in which the opposition gains power, so that there is not the sense of a sudden unprepared need to respond post-election to a new regime. And even in circumstances where there is an initial degree of mistrust, as in three of the examples discussed in this chapter, there is much a skilled chief executive can do to overcome resistance and to begin to develop a productive relationship (even from the most unpromising of beginnings). In extremis, however, a chief executive may decide his or her position is no longer tenable and that a new post elsewhere should be sought.

6
The Chief Executive as a Political Animal

Introduction

It is axiomatic that chief executives must become immersed in the world of politics, as it operates in their authorities: they could not operate effectively if they were not. Several important dimensions of this immersion have already been emphasised; understanding the (party) political dynamics of the authority; understanding where the leader is coming from politically (and his or her standing within the party group and executive); building bridges to opposition groups; supporting new leaders who are struggling with their role; and (where appropriate) exchanging information about the internal dynamics of party group and management team respectively. All these are ways of picking up relevant political information – or responding to it – and would generally be regarded as uncontentious.

Yet one or two of the examples of chief executive behaviour discussed in earlier chapters indicate a rather more contentious 'political' role for chief executives; the way one chief executive bargained with a party leader in a (successful) attempt to persuade him to agree to the idea of 'political assistants'; and the way another chief executive provided information and support to a councillor who was challenging for the leadership of a party group (and, by implication, of the council).

As we shall see in this chapter, the interviews revealed several more examples of chief executives behaving in ways which other chief executives might regard as inappropriate. Why inappropriate? Because there is a broad agreement 'in principle' in most local authorities that the political leadership deals with the party political side of the council's operations, whilst the chief executive deals with the managerial side, the leader/chief executive relationship providing the essential conduit between the two worlds (paralleled by a set of cabinet member/chief officer relationships). From this perspective the behaviour of a chief executive who supported and briefed one leadership contender (but not others) could be seen as an unwarranted intrusion into a world that should be left exclusively to the political group concerned.

The principle of mutual separation of managerial and political worlds can be breached (and often is) in other ways. We have already seen how the 'members make policy officers implement it' maxim is sometimes disregarded. Chief executives (and other chief officers) sometimes in effect 'make policy', which members agree, and then seek ways of becoming involved in its implementation. It is a general principle not a hard and fast rule (see Chapter 10 for further discussion). In this chapter, it is the involvement of a chief executive in the task of maintaining a stable and cohesive political environment that is the main focus of discussion.

Whilst acknowledging the inevitability of a degree of political uncertainty that an election-based system of representative democracy inevitably brings, it is in the interests of both a council leader and chief executive to do as much as they can to ensure a stable political environment, or perhaps more realistically to avoid an unstable political environment (with the level of uncertainty that this entails). Particularly in terms of long-term planning, chief executives are advantaged if they can anticipate with some confidence that key decisions which contribute to the council's strategy are not going to be reversed arbitrarily. Unstable alliances in hung authorities, or internally divided majority groups, are particular threats to this stability. Similarly leaders will want to do as much as they can to maintain and strengthen their position in the face of such threats (or more generally). There is thus a common interest between leader and chief executive, assuming they have a reasonably good working relationship, to seek to secure, or to sustain a stable decision-making environment, within the limits of the possible.

There are various ways in which chief executives can be drawn into the political world (and hence operate as political animals) which go beyond the relatively uncontentious activities listed at the start of this chapter. Sometimes it is a case of a chief executive being drawn into the political world at the behest of a leader, sometimes the intrusion is instigated by the chief executive.

Here are some examples from the research. Chief executives have been faced with requests from leaders to help with drafting their party manifesto, to discipline an errant cabinet colleague, to attend a party group meeting, and to provide advice as to who should be the cabinet. One was also faced with a demand from a council leader that he should attend management team meetings on a regular basis.

Chief executives have volunteered advice on possible coalitions in a hung authority, have put pressure on leaders to sort out the council budget in a civilised way, have strongly advised against political intentions that they regard as 'bad for the area', have urged the leader to take disciplinary action in relation to colleagues, and have sought to help leaders strengthen their position within the group (they have also in particular cases helped a leadership contender in his leadership bid). All these examples raise issues about the legitimate role of a chief executive in what would normally be seen as 'political' activities.

Some of these examples are rarely found or are relatively easily dealt with when they do occur. It is only the occasional idiosyncratic leader who now feels it necessary or desirable to attend management team meetings. Experienced chief executives would be likely to find ways of dissuading them. The problem for one chief executive interviewee who'd experienced this pressure was her inexperience.

> *Soon after I was appointed, the leader insisted on attending management team meetings.... I was too inexperienced then to tell him it wasn't appropriate... but I certainly would now, if faced with the same situation.*

Similarly the attendance of chief executives at party group meetings, although not uncommon, is rarely contentious, so long as opportunities are offered to all parties represented and the 'rules of engagement' are clear. However, occasional embarrassments have occurred.

> *At one Liberal Democrat group meeting, the leader praised me as 'someone who gives me better political advice than I get from the*

group'.... I had to intervene quickly to make clear the nature of the advice which I provided.

The role of the chief executive as whistleblower – either directly or through the monitoring officer if the chief executive does not hold this position – may be uncomfortable, but it is a legally enshrined role which in principle has to be accepted by party leaders. Nevertheless there is reluctance on the part of some chief executives to apply this role, in circumstances where in principle it might be justified, because of the potential damage to the relationship with the leader.

It is not uncommon for a chief executive to be faced with the situation where there is evidence that the behaviour or misdemeanours of a cabinet colleague of the leader makes his or her position as cabinet member untenable, and the leader has to be persuaded of the need to dispense with their services. The question is then raised of who should tell the cabinet member concerned that they have to go.

In 2002 one of the cabinet was convicted of assaulting his carer.... I immediately contacted the leader and said 'you have to sack this guy from the cabinet' – which fortunately he did.

Soon after I was appointed I realised that three or four committee chairs needed to be strongly encouraged to step down...there was evidence of expenses fiddling and, in one case someone with a history of child abuse...action should really have been taken by the leader, but he asked me to do it...with some reluctance, I did, because it was so important for the reputation of the authority.

The pressure on a chief executive to advise on the selection of cabinet colleagues is rare, and dangerous for a chief executive to comply with, as an interviewee in the 2005 JRF research recognised.

The leader asked for my advice about what changes should be made in his cabinet. There was no way I was going to do this.... I know that if I did, the leader would tell those he'd sacked that it was at my suggestion.

The three situations which raised the most serious questions about the chief executive's political role were contribution to manifestos;

involvement in the formation of an administration in a hung authority; and attempts to persuade a leader to do (or not do) something which was (or was not) in the interests of the authority or the area.

Chief executives and party manifestos

It should be clear from what has already been written that chief executives vary considerably in the extent to which they become involved in issues which would be seen as 'party political' in nature. A good illustration of this variation is provided by one of the most 'political' chief executives amongst the interviewees.

> *I have always been prepared to offer advice to parties on the drafting of their manifestos ... not on what they should do, but more along the lines of 'is what you are suggesting feasible?' or 'is there a better way of expressing your aspirations?' ... in 2006 the Liberal Democrats took advantage of this offer, and I had a real influence on the way the manifesto was presented.*

Other chief executives would not have dreamt of providing a manifesto advice in such a detailed way (or indeed at all), although there is a 'middle ground' of responding to specific enquiries raised by a political group in particular circumstances.

> *As part of the recovery plan (from a poor CPA result) the Labour leadership wanted to consult me about their manifesto – not the content, but rather how it should be taken forward and prioritised, so that we could demonstrate a capacity for recovery ...*

The problem is what the response of other parties would be if they were to hear about the help a chief executive had provided to their political opponents. In the CPA-linked example, it was virtually certain that Labour would continue to form the administration after the forthcoming election (albeit on a minority basis). In the first example, the chief executive emphasised that he offered help to all three parties (although the other two had not taken up the offer) and that if his contribution to the Liberal Democrat manifesto became widely known 'it wouldn't have been a problem'. Maybe not; but the kind of involvement which had taken place has to be managed extremely carefully – it could be seen as moving into a dangerous confusion of political/managerial roles.

Dealing with a hung situation

The main problem occurs when the move to no overall control is unexpected. Authorities that have a long experience of no overall control normally develop mechanisms for dealing with the situation (sometimes enshrined as protocols, but more typically as informal rules, e.g. that the largest party is expected to form a minority administration). It is the unexpected onset of hungness that forces chief executives to 'think on their feet' and to seek to facilitate a workable outcome.

Again there are a range of different responses ranging from a view that the dilemma of what to do is a political one, in which the chief executive should play no part, to the unashamedly proactive role played by a chief executive in 1984 (Leach and Stewart 1992, p. 95).

> In one hung MDC in 1984, where the Conservatives had previously been in majority control, the chief executive exhorted the leader of the Conservative group to form a minority administration 'for the good of the district'.

More typically, the terms used by chief executives to describe what they do are those of 'honest broker', or intermediary. However, there are two distinctive interpretations of this role; one where the chief executive makes himself or herself available for one-to-one meetings with party leaders, and the other where he or she is prepared to act as a de facto 'messenger' relaying information as to possible viable options from one party leader to another.

The distinction was recognised and commented on by one interviewee.

> *My position (in a hung council) is that I will emphasise the need for the party group to reach some kind of outcome...but I won't seek to broker an agreement.... I see myself as a catalyst, not a broker.... I'll bring leaders together collectively or respond to requests for individual meetings but I won't seek proactively to influence the different groups.*

A particularly difficult hung situation faced by another chief executive was dealt with on a similar basis.

> the first meeting with the leaders was awful – the Labour leader stormed out... after which I realised it would be impossible to resolve the issue at a leaders meeting.... I then acted as a 'go-between' (not a power broker) making it clear that I had no preferred option of my own.... I kept relaying messages between the three leaders, until it became clear that a Liberal Democrat/Conservative coalition was the only feasible option...

Sometimes chief executives have to be forthright about the need for the parties to reach some kind of outcome (typically referred to as 'banging heads together').

> I told them then I didn't care what type of administration they formed, as long as they agreed on something.

Interesting the same chief executive acknowledged that he reserved the right to move into a broker's role, had this become necessary.

> I would have provided confidential advice about the feasibility of the option (that eventually emerged) to leaders... or indeed any other option, if I'd been asked to do so.

Before 2000, when there was no legal requirement to form an administration one chief executive used the tactic of saying she would 'run the authority herself', which had the desired effect.

> After the 1997 elections, none of the parties could reach agreement... so I said 'right, I'll run the authority'... faced with this outcome, Labour and the Liberal Democrats agreed to take the chairs.

The more proactive 'brokerage' role is illustrated by the following example.

> When the authority became hung, I rang each group leader to say that I was happy to help in the formation of an administration.... I operated as a facilitator in the emergence of a minority Labour administration,

> *primarily through briefing the Labour leader that the Liberal Democrats saw this as an acceptable outcome.*

An interview from the earlier JRF research (2005) identified an even more proactive chief executive role, this time in ensuring the smooth running of the authority.

> I see my main job in the hung situation as acting as inter-party broker. I have regular one-to-one meetings with the Council Leader (Labour), the Conservative leader and the Green party leader. At the meetings with the opposition party leaders I try and gauge their likely positions on key decisions which are coming up.... this enables me to feedback information to the council leader as to whether Labour will get their recommendation through... or whether they'll struggle.

A pertinent question here is why it was the chief executive who was playing this party brokerage role rather than the council leader?

The danger of the brokerage role is that if it becomes clear to the party which is ultimately excluded that the chief executive has operated in this kind of way, it may (with some justification) cause the party to feel that he or she has disadvantaged them, with implications for future mistrust and (in the event of the group gaining power) a judgement that the chief executive should be replaced. It is a 'high risk' strategy which stretches to the limit (and perhaps beyond) the circumstances in which a chief executive can legitimately operate in a political sphere.

The chief executive as a moral arbiter – 'in the interests of the area'

The traditional view is that, if presented with a political agenda which is within the bounds of legality, a chief executive should strive to deliver it (within of course, the financial constraints within which the authority operates). That view was accepted by all the interviewees; indeed in some cases the problem was identifying a political agenda to seek to deliver. However, some of the chief executives interviewed made a significant qualification to this general view, revealing that there were occasions where they had argued strongly that a (legal) course of action, favoured by the political leadership, was *not* a good idea, or, alternatively, that a course of action not favoured by the leadership *should* be pursued, 'for the good of the area'.

There were two different reasons for interventions of this kind. First there were occasions when chief executives cited 'the reputation of the authority' as a reason for politicians to behave (or to stop behaving) in a particular way. Secondly there was intervention in relation to particular decisions or policies.

Intervention on behavioural grounds is exemplified by the chief executive of a hung council who, horrified at the climate of the first council budget-setting meeting she witnessed, determined to prevent a recurrence the following year.

> *I insisted that they got their act together before the formal budget-setting meeting in February in the meeting the previous year had been chaotic. It had shown the authority in a very bad light and the local press had made the most of it...*

Similar interventions were identified in relation to dealing with the onset of a no overall control situation, and in seeking to dissuade a Conservative member from introducing a 'notice of motion' which the chief executive knew would inflame the opposition unnecessarily. Also in relation to partnership working it was sometimes felt that the political attitudes displayed were both impolite and counterproductive.

> *I've had to push the importance of partnership with the Labour group which certainly wasn't, at first, supportive of the idea and tended to behave inappropriately to the other representatives at partnership meetings.*

In other words, the chief executive's message was that they may not have rated partnership working, but that in her view it was indeed important. It should of course be recognised that there are valid political reasons for council leaders to challenge the concept of partnership in this way given their perception that partnership-working is undermining the traditional 'sovereign' role of the council.

In a sense there is nothing untoward about a chief executive seeking to persuade party groups (through their leaders) to modify their behaviour, although there may be an issue of judgement as to how far a point of view can be pushed, if there is initial political resistance, without detriment to the future relationship with the leader(s) concerned. The same point is true of chief executives seeking to dissuade a political leader from a particular course of action (or to persuade him or her to take one). Chief executives have long operated in this way. But it should be recognised that what chief executives are doing here is seeking to influence a political agenda, and there is an important issue about how far this kind of 'attempt to influence' can be taken. Are there occasions where it can (or should) become a 'bottom line' issue – a case for resignation?

The legitimacy of a chief executive seeking forcefully to influence politicians in this way was illustrated eloquently by one interviewee.

> It's not enough for a chief executive to consider the legality and administrative feasibility of a political agenda before acting on it. It's also important to consider whether what is proposed is beneficial – or detrimental – to the quality of life in the council's area...

The chief executive cited an example from an authority in which he had previously worked, in which a recently elected leader wanted to cancel proposals for two major developments in the town centre, and to use the land for extra car-parking.

> The town needed new development to become a more attractive, competitive centre. If the schemes were cancelled there would be no point in introducing more car parking... indeed the use of existing car parks was well below capacity... I would have done all I could to convince the leader of the illogicality of his proposals... and would probably have resigned if I'd failed... because it was a moral issue...

Other cases cited included strong encouragement for a leader to identify an eco-town site in the authority (ultimately unsuccessful) and a major challenge to a leader's opposition to 'a planning application which would have been of major benefit to the area, because of some very minor environmental concerns he had'.

An interviewee from the 2005 JRF research used the 'morality' metaphor in a rather different way.

My main task has been to 'save the soul' of the council... by standing up to the leader... and seeking to protect its core values and its integrity.

Such cases raise an interesting issue of the extent to which the adoption of a 'moral' position can be justified. In the case of the 'town centre development versus car-parks' example, would it have made a difference if the new leader had presented a rather different argument, along the lines that he didn't want the town centre to experience major development, because that would adversely affect its character and the quality of its environment? In that case there would have been two viable competing views about 'the good of the area'. What (arguably) justified the chief executive's view was the illogicality of using the freed-up land for car parks which would clearly not be needed.

There are undoubtedly dangers in chief executives taking a moral 'benefit of the area' line, unless they are very sure of their ground. One can see how the argument could be used to dissuade an inexperienced new administration from introducing a policy which (in terms of its own values) could be argued to be of benefit to the area. It is of course legitimate for a chief executive to make any 'arguments against' that he or she feels are needed to make to enable politicians to reach a balanced view. However, the fact that politicians have a democratic mandate which chief executives lack means that the final judgement in such cases should be theirs. It is doubtful whether there are more than one or two circumstances in which 'moral' arguments (such as the example cited above) can reasonably be persisted with and used as a justification for resignation.

The more a chief executive moves beyond the informal (traditional) limits to 'political involvement', the more he or she risks embarrassment. The chief executive who was thanked by his leader for providing 'better political advice' than the party group provides one example. Another chief executive volunteered an illustration from a time when she held a deputy chief executive position.

At a particular council meeting opposition members said, when challenging the council leadership 'well, the deputy chief executive told us...'. I quickly set up a meeting with the opposition leader and told him that this wasn't on... it's absolutely right to give opposition

> *members a proper briefing, particularly in an authority which changes control on a regular basis...but if I'm to do this, I can't risk being exposed in public in that way...basically I had to say 'please don't you ever do that again'...*

The implication is that if a chief executive (or deputy) is to provide helpful support to political leaders which goes beyond normal expectations, there is an implied 'quid pro quo' that the beneficiaries do not cause embarrassment by being too explicit about their sources, a situation which illustrates the importance of informal 'shared understandings' with all political groups, if chief executives are to operate effectively.

7
The Essence of a Good Relationship

'Good leaders' and 'bad leaders'

The qualities which chief executives interviewed sought and often found in leaders can be summarised in the following 'composite' cameo ('The Good Leader'). The antitheses of these qualities are summarised in the second cameo ('The Bad Leader'). This material is familiar from other recent studies, such as the SOLACE report (2006). However, listing desirable qualities is one thing; stimulating them when they are absent is another! A more challenging agenda for chief executives is how the desired qualities can be generated (if not already in existence) and how 'problem' characteristics can be overcome. This agenda takes a chief executive into the world of negotiation (and sometimes bargaining) and requires personal relationship skills (discussed in Chapters 4 and 5), at which some chief executives are clearly better equipped than others.

The Good Leader

The 'good leader' is one who possesses a long-term time horizon and a clear set of strategic priorities, but does not interfere (except in extremis) in the implementation of those priorities, or the management of the authority. Good leaders have the capacity to persuade their groups to follow their lead, once something has been agreed with the chief executive – or at least to be clear about when they can and when they can't guarantee

(Continued)

this outcome. They are prepared to confront difficult choices and have frank and open discussions about these choices. Good leaders are flexible; they are prepared to negotiate and compromise to make progress. They are good communicators who can (ideally) 'talk the same language' as the chief executive. They are reliable, honest and consistent in their dealings and do not spring surprises on the chief executive. Their judgement is sound. They operate on a 'no surprises' basis. In these circumstances the probability of the development of a relationship which embodies mutual trust and mutual respect is high.

The list of desired qualities in chief executives from the perspective of leaders (see SOLACE report 2006, p. 28) is similar but with some predictable differences. For example chief executives are favoured who

- are politically realistic – sometimes decisions are taken which are not professionally obvious
- understand politics and politicians, and can work with the political process
- understand the problems and look for solutions, rather than merely defend the traditional process
- are in touch with the real world – aware of how policy is playing 'out there'.

In contrast to the good leader, the bad leader possesses a series of qualities (and lacks others) which can make life very difficult for a chief executive.

The Bad Leader

Bad leaders do not think strategically, their focus is on short-term problems of service delivery. They have a tendency to interfere in management/ implementation issues which should be the responsibility of officers. They are politically naïve or weak – being unable in many circumstances to sense the

> climate of opinion in their group or to persuade the group of a desirable course of action. Bad leaders are often inflexible; once they have made up their minds (often on the basis of superficial evidence) it is very difficult to persuade them to reconsider. They can be inconsistent and unreliable, agreeing a course of action with a chief executive, and then not taking it forward. They spring surprises on chief executives in public settings (which should have been discussed privately beforehand) and are prone to 'temper tantrums' both in private and (particularly problematical for a chief executive) in public. Their judgement is often suspect and the probability of the development of a relationship which embodies mutual trust and respect is low.

In reality of course, it is unlikely that the chief executive would find himself or herself working with a leader with the full range of desirable qualities (although there were chief executives who described leaders with whom they had worked as being close to this ideal picture). Similarly a chief executive would be extremely unlikely to be faced with a leader with the full range of 'unhelpful' qualities set out in the second cameo (although again one or two chief executives reported experiences with leaders who exhibited a high proportion of them!) In such cases a long-term relationship is unlikely – either the leader is deposed or the chief executive moves on. Much more typical is the situation where a chief executive is faced with a leader with some positive qualities and some more problematical characteristics (as seen from the chief executive's perspective). The interesting question then is 'what can be done'? How far can the relationship be managed in a way which steers it in the direction of the ideal?

All you need is trust?

A previous piece of research by the author on member–officer relations (Leach, Pratchett and Wingfield (1997)) was entitled 'All you need is trust?' The title was intended to be ironic (hence the question mark). It became quite clear to the research team during the course of the project that whereas 'trust' was an extremely helpful – indeed some would argue essential – quality in leader/chief executive relationships, it was by no means 'all you need'. A clarity in the division of responsibilities was equally desirable. Our interviews in 1997 were permeated by leaders and chief executives emphasising the importance of trust. This quality was also much referred to in the interviews which formed the basis for this book. Of course trust is important, but how does a chief executive set about generating (or strengthening) trust, and what does he or she do when faced with a leader who demonstrates a lack of trustworthiness, and no apparent appetite for change?

There will be many instances where the starting point is distinctly unpromising. In Chapter 5, three examples were proved of chief executives faced with newly elected leaders who were not predisposed to trust them (see pp. 65–8). In each case, after a difficult few months, the leaders involved did begin to trust the chief executives involved (in part due to some good judgements made by the chief executives about what (and when) to challenge and not to challenge in the early stages of the relationship).

But other chief executives interviewed found it much more difficult to generate even an adequate level of trust. A chief executive from the earlier JRF research (2005) explained his dilemma in the following terms.

> ... the leader was utterly untrustworthy ... he told the truth 80 per cent of the time and lied 20 per cent – the problem was you didn't know which 20 per cent...!

Even when a chief executive has been appointed by a leader (not solely by a leader, but a leader's view is always crucial in a chief executive appointment) there is no guarantee that a requisite level of trust will develop. One chief executive did his best to resolve a problem which became apparent a few months after his appointment (the leader had agreed that his group would withdraw from micromanagement, but did not do so, following a successful election).

> *I made various attempts to resolve the problem....I brought in outsiders to help mediate...in each case I tried to get the leader to agree to a way of working which would enable me to continue...sometimes he appeared to agree, but didn't carry out his side of the agreement...sometimes he tried later to change the terms of the agreement in ways I found unacceptable.*

Not surprisingly, having tried and failed to build the requisite degree of trust with the leader, this chief executive decided he could not continue in the post.

The implications of this example (and there were others identified by interviewees) is that there will be some situations where it just is not possible to develop the level of mutual trust necessary to make the relationship sustainable. Most of the chief executives interviewed had however managed to build at least an acceptable level of trust. But a couple of chief executives recognised that even when this outcome had been achieved, it was important not to become complacent. Examples were cited of other chief executives who had appeared to enjoy a good working relationship with their leader, only for it to fall apart unexpectedly. 'Keep working at it' was the advice of one chief executive. Another put it like this.

> *You mustn't get complacent about a good working relationship with a leader... you mustn't let it stagnate... you've got to keep reviewing it and challenging it as circumstances change.*

The importance of negotiation

Negotiation is the key to a good chief executive/leader relationship. If a number of potentially difficult areas can be identified, discussed and resolved, then there is the basis (all other things being equal) for a good working relationship. The key areas for negotiation', which became apparent as the sequences of interviews progressed, can be summarised as follows:

- Exchange of information and advice – what, when and how?
- Dealing with conflicts/differences of view
- Ensuring clarity of role differentiation
- Managing the personal relationship – 'close but not too close'.

Exchange of information and advice

Several chief executives argued that in an era characterised by a stream of central government initiatives and a proliferation of inspectoral regimes (not to mention the increasing need to become involved in regional and sub-regional machinery) the challenge of keeping the leader properly briefed had increased in importance and became more time-consuming. What leaders 'needed to know' was more extensive than it had been 10 years ago. The principle of 'no surprises' – widely espoused by leaders and chief executives alike – referred not just to 'bad news' items (see below) but included anything that a leader might be asked to comment on or respond to, within party group, council or local media.

For this reason, most chief executives had instigated a weekly briefing meeting with the leader, at which a range of such matters could be discussed (including of course items which the leader wished to raise with the chief executive, although it is usually the latter who is the dominant force in setting the agenda). A problem for some chief executives was a disinclination on the part of a leader for this programmed approach. Some leaders prefer to 'drop in' in the chief executive on a relatively informal (and often not pre-arranged) basis. In the light of the widely-held view that chief executives have to adjust to the behaviour and preference of leaders, rather than vice versa, it is not surprising that chief executives find ways of adjusting to this more unstructured pattern. There is also the problem of the ease with which some leaders become bored (the 'short attention span' syndrome) in which case there is a challenge for the chief executive to get the main points across as economically as possible. (see examples on Chapter 4, p. 58).

In other cases, particularly perhaps in counties, there is an opportunity provided by shared car journeys to provide informal briefings. There is thus a judgement to be made by chief executives as to how best to achieve the objective of keeping the leader properly briefed, in the context of the behavioural patterns and preferences of the leaders.

In the SOLACE report (2006, p. 34) it is observed that chief executives may, in certain circumstances, be blamed for 'bad news', for example a new government requirement that is an anathema politically to the dominant group. If requisite levels of trust, openness and honesty have developed in the relationship, it is highly unlikely that the leader would apportion blame in this way. The possibility only really exists if the relationship is in difficulty anyway. Thus one chief executive struggling to maintain a workable relationship with a 'difficult' leader made the following point.

> *I don't subscribe to the view that there are certain things you should keep from members... my view is that if they 'need to know' something*

you have to tell them, even if the news is unpalatable...it would be worse if they weren't told, but subsequently found out from another source...I have been blamed as the bearer of bad news...but sometimes you've just got to be brave.

The 'no surprises' principle can be breached by leaders as well as chief executives. One chief executive was given no prior warning about the possible removal of the whip from the council leader by the Labour group. Another had to remonstrate with a council leader who made a statement in public which in effect breached council policy, without forewarning the chief executive.

The cabinet had endorsed a policy which involved a reconfiguration of library provision, including several closures...the following week the leader made a public statement that one of the proposed closures would not go ahead....I raised this problem with him at our next weekly meeting and said that there would have to be a report to cabinet about what was in effect a change of policy...he was clearly very uneasy about the whole business...

'Exchange of information' can extend beyond substantive issues facing the council. Three interviewees explained how useful it was to work with a leader who was prepared to discuss tensions within his or her group (the 'quid pro quo' was that the chief executive was expected to be equally open about the management team).

I brief the leader about any significant developments in the management team, and in return, he briefs me about currents of opinion within his group...this is very helpful information, but we both take great care to ensure that the exchanges remain confidential.

Over time, our discussions came to include the leader's problems with his group, and mine with the management team. Neither was strictly necessary, but it gave us both a lot of useful insights.

Leader/chief executive briefing meetings do not of course only include the exchange of information. They also invariably involve an opportunity, on the chief executive's part, for giving informal advice – 'this is what I think we should do'. For example in 2006, having learned of the government's intention to provide an opportunity for authorities to bid for unitary status, chief executives typically were keen that the opportunity should be taken.

> *I was keen that we should make a bid for unitary status ... the leader agreed, but then received an edict from Central Office that Conservative-controlled counties were not to make bids ...*

A crucial element of a good relationship, from a chief executive's perspective, is the freedom to present options to leaders in an unrestricted way, accepting that a chief executive's preferred option may be rejected.

> *It's been so important to be allowed to present options to the leadership and to argue for ones' preferences .... I would find it very hard to work in an authority where the advice you gave to leaders was constrained in any way ...*

Other chief executives stressed the importance of feeling free to draw the leader's attention to new opportunities, in circumstances where they knew that a leader's initial reaction was unlikely to be supportive.

> *The DCLG contacted us to see if we were prepared to identify an eco-town site .... I was very enthusiastic about the idea – there was a lot of government money involved ... the leader was at first very much against the idea, but I tried hard to persuade him ... 'why are you against it? Have you considered the benefits' ... ?*

In this case the leader was not persuaded (and indeed there were valid counter arguments) but at least was prepared to allow the chief executive to make a (persistent) case.

Dealing with conflict

It is inevitable that, even in the best of leader/chief executive relationships, differences of opinion will emerge from time to time which have the potential, if both parties hold their views strongly, of developing into conflict. Such tensions and potential conflicts often reflect the differences between 'political' and 'managerial' imperatives, discussed in Chapter 1. What seems good from a political perspective may be seen as thoroughly bad from a managerial perspective, and vice versa. What is important is not to seek to prevent such tensions developing (they are inevitable) but to have effective mechanisms for resolving them when they do occur.

Several chief executives stressed the crucial importance of knowing that they can confront the leader and express disagreement or disapproval in private (although certainly not in public). The capacity to do so may be regarded as an essential component of a good relationship.

> *The leader sometimes has a go at me in a cabinet meeting, for reasons that make sense to him politically, and which I understand, but I don't think it's OK behaviour... however our relationship is strong enough for me to express my displeasure (in private) to him afterwards.*

> *we quickly established that it was OK for me to stand up to the leader and challenge him when I felt it was appropriate... for example at a partnership meeting the leader made an intervention which I thought was unhelpful and out of character... after the meeting, I took him to one side and said 'what was all that about'?*

A similar example, which proved crucial for the future of the relationship, is that cited earlier (see Chapter 3) where a chief executive told his leader that he thought the way the latter had treated a management team member was unacceptable.

The examples set out above, important though they are, are about behavioural issues. More problematic are disagreements about policies or decisions. Several chief executives used the term 'I had to put my foot down' to characterise issues of this nature. These are often 'bottom line' issues, which could, if unresolved, cause the chief executive to consider resignation.

> *It's important to make it clear to leaders when you think they intend to do something inappropriate... one leader I worked with wanted to influence the letting of a contract, not for personal gain, but because he had developed a strong preference for one contractor... I had to warn him, in no uncertain terms, that he had to distance himself...*

> *The leader wanted some action in his ward that wasn't covered by policy. I had to tell him that what he wanted wasn't possible... but I agreed to*

> *try to find a different way of achieving what he wanted ... which in the end I did.*

The last response illustrates a predisposition on the part of many chief executives to minimise the situations in which they have to say a straight 'no'. The preference is to try to find a way of responding to the leaders concern in a different way to the one he or she had initially proposed.

Other examples of chief executives taking a strong line cover issues such as 'you must avoid the chaos of last year's budget meeting and the harm it did to the council's reputation' (see Chapter 6, p. 79) and 'you must sort out a way of responding to no overall control' (see Chapter 6, p. 77).

There are also times when a chief executive will encourage a leader to confront difficult choices, and regard it as a strength if the leader is prepared to do so.

> *The leader has always been prepared to confront and deal with difficult choices ... there was a development proposal which was of great potential advantage to the area, but which involved the demolition of a group of council houses. The previous administration had ducked the issue ... the new leader listened to my views, decided it was worth doing and made it happen politically, despite the public opposition he knew would be involved.*

Ensuring clarity of role definition

The concern about an overemphasis on 'partnership' in the way certain chief executives characterise their relationships with leaders is that it can, in certain circumstances, reflect a *blurring* of roles; a lack of clarity about the dividing line between the political and managerial. Some of the chief executives interviews were well aware of this danger.

> *There is a clear differentiation in our profiles ... the leader does all the external stuff and does it well .... I play much more of a 'backroom support' role than I did when the authority was hung, and am much happier with that.*

> *You need to be clear about the complementary nature of the leader and chief executive roles ... and not compete for the same space.*

There is a problem for chief executives who are pushed into roles which they themselves regard as more appropriate for a leader to play. In the earlier (JRF 2005) research one chief executive explained a dilemma of this nature.

> There is a problem about our respective profiles. I am too often seen as the strong central figure. The local paper had an article recently about our 'good' CPA result ... with a picture of me rather than the leader ... the press seem to enjoy talking to me rather too much, as far as the leader is concerned ...

The response of one chief executive to this situation is revealing.

> *I find it absolutely amazing that a chief executive could put him or herself in a position where effectively the council leader is denied good press publicity ...*

Whilst the principles of 'clear division of roles and responsibilities' and 'not competing for the same space' gained widespread (although not universal) support, there remains the challenge of negotiating just what the division of labour should be. This process is often a difficult one, as is illustrated in Chapter 10, where we discuss this issue in relation to the pressures of the CPA inspection process. There was often an acknowledgement of the need for flexibility, as illustrated by quotes from the JRF (2005) interview.

> There must be a clear dividing-line between member involvement and officer involvement in decision-making. As chief executive it's up to me to maintain that line. The dividing-line is movable, but it has to be there – without it, there's chaos.

> The mayor and I both know there's a line between what he should be doing and what I should be doing. There are times when I allow him to cross that line, but I ensure that he knows that that's what I'm doing.

Managing the personal relationship

The maxim 'close but not too close' was widely seen as appropriate as the preferred basis of leader/chief executive relationships. It was helpful if the two parties 'got on well' in personal terms, could 'speak the same language' and shared some similar external interests (and a sense of humour). But there were dangers, not least in the event of a change in political control, if the relationship came to be perceived as 'too close', with the implication of disappointment on the chief executive's part if the leader lost power.

> *The relationship has to be close, but not too cosy... the leader and I don't socialise outside of the county council commitments, and I wouldn't think it was appropriate if we did.*

Another chief executive (JRF 2005 research) made a similar point.

> *I've known the leader since 1985. We are neither friends nor enemies. I've never had a drink with him – that's not the way it works. But I do understand his politics and his personality and he understands the way I work...*

There are sometimes opportunities for the leader (or chief executive) to respond sympathetically to a personal crisis in other's life, in a way which strengthens the relationship, without breaching the 'close but not too close' principle.

> *In my previous authority, when my husband became seriously ill, the leader, who had previously been 'undemonstrative' in the way he dealt with me, became extremely supportive, including coping with me bursting into tears... I think the episode was helpful – it showed them I was human...*

Another chief executive experienced a degree of sympathy from the leader in response to the news of the break-up of her marriage, in a way that she too appreciated and found beneficial to the quality of the relationship.

All four of the key areas of negotiation discussed in this chapter are important for leaders and chief executives to resolve, either directly (through early discussion) or more gradually, as issues arise within them that require clarification or resolution. Such issues can be crucial in influencing the future course and quality of the relationship as the following example illustrates.

> *Soon after I was appointed to my first chief executive job... the leader shouted at me in public in a hotel foyer, in front of the leaders and chief executives of all the districts (in the county).... I turned to face him and said, 'Right, I'm leaving' and stormed out.... I assumed that was the end of my job in that authority and I had already began to pack my things in the office the next day, when the leader rang – in tears and hugely apologetic...*

The leader had breached the unwritten but widely-accepted rule that chief executives and leaders should not criticise each other in public arenas. Whenever the rule is breached (almost always by leaders) it invariably leads to direct confrontation of the leader by the chief executive to seek assurances that the behaviour will not recur. If it does recur, it may result in the resignation on the part of the chief executive (it is typically symptomatic of wider problems).

The process of negotiation, however conducted, can be seen as an attempt to develop a shared understanding of the 'rules of the game' without which a productive relationship would be extremely difficult. Several chief executives in doing so emphasised the need to 'keep talking' about a problem, on a face-to-face basis (there was unease about the use of e-mails in such situations – they were a tempting way of making a quick response, but were vulnerable to 'second thoughts' the next day!)

> *If there is a falling out or misunderstanding, the important thing is to talk about it right away, to try to resolve it, and learn from it so that the problem can be avoided in future.*

Conclusion

The essence of good relationship on the evidence of the interviews is that it should contain most (ideally all) of the following qualities.

- a capacity for information exchange which extends beyond briefing the leader on what he or she needs to know to a mutual

exchange of 'soft' information about the dynamics of executive and management team respectively
- the existence of effective mechanisms for identifying and resolving differences of view and (potential) conflicts between leader and chief executive
- a clear differentiation of respective roles and responsibilities, based on a mutual appreciation of the key differences between the 'political' and the 'managerial'...but a degree of flexibility in the application of the agreed guidelines
- an avoidance of personal criticism of each other in public arenas
- a friendly personal relationship 'close but not too close'.

Probably the most challenging of these desiderata is the third (role differentiation) which can impact on the second (the need for conflict resolution mechanisms) a topic which provides the main focus of the next chapter.

8
Testing the Relationship

The functional – or dysfunctional – nature of the relationship between chief executive and leader becomes apparent when it is 'tested' by the occurrence of a 'critical incident'. Critical incidents are 'unexpected' happenings which challenge the nature of the relationship, either through the fact that one or other of the participants in 'breaking the rules' (typically unwritten in nature) *or* there are no rules or guidelines to assist the resolution of an issue over which leader and chief executive have different views.

Critical incidents provide a test which, if resolved to the mutual satisfaction of both parties, can actually strengthen the relationship. On the other hand, if the issue is not resolved satisfactorily, it leaves a residue of unease which can undermine the relationship, particularly if further critical incidents occur with similar outcomes.

In the interviews carried out for this book, I asked each chief executive if they could identify 'critical incidents' in their current or previous chief executive jobs. All were able to do so, and the following discussion is based on an analysis of 50 such incidents,[1] some of which have already been alluded to in previous chapters.

The critical incidents identified can be allocated to six different categories as listed in Table 8.1.

Establishing credibility by decisive action

Instances of the first category of critical incidents do not appear critical at the time (in that chief executives and leaders do not have to confront each other and resolve a divisive issue) but they can have a

Table 8.1 Categories of critical incidents

		Examples[2]
(1)	Establishing credibility by decisive action	4
(2)	Management issues – defending valued colleagues against pressures for dismissal or seeking help to ease out problematical colleagues	6
(3)	Seeking to persuade leaders to do something they don't favour … or to dissuade them from doing something felt to be inappropriate … or to persuade them of the need for decisive action	14
(4)	Dealing with inappropriate or challenging behaviour from a leader in public or private settings	14
(5)	Coping with difficult situations reflecting the political circumstances of authority (in some cases resulting from misjudgements by the chief executive)	9
(6)	Dealing with 'bad news' that may be seen to reflect badly on the chief executive	3

profound effect on the future quality of a relationship. Mention was made in Chapter 4 of the newly appointed chief executive who made a point of seeking out the opposition leader after she had (unfairly in his view) been subjected to virulent criticism from the then leader in the council chamber. That action established his credibility with the opposition group, and its leader, who a year later became council leader (of a minority Labour administration) herself. A similar (but different) example of an influential exchange between a chief executive and a future leader is provided below.

> On the day I was appointed, I got an angry phone call from the leader (then a backbencher) who told me he thought my appointment was a disgrace, because my Labour party sympathies were well-known. I stood up to him and he backed down.

The chief executive's response established his credibility with a future leader, in a way which proved very helpful (although could not, of course, have been foreseen at the time).

Another chief executive who at one point in his career was brought in, on a temporary basis, to a 'failing authority' to help to turn it round, dealt with a difficult situation at a Recovery Board meeting in a way which proved significant.

> *A head of service was given a dressing-down at a meeting by one of Board – quite unfairly in my view. I made a point of seeking out the officer concerned and told how unhappy I was at the way he had been treated. I also contacted the Board member concerned and told him I wanted him to resign...*

The support given to the officer concerned, which of course he shared with his colleagues, gave the chief executive a lot of credibility with senior staff in his endeavours to change the authority's culture.

Another chief executive described a situation where she felt she had to act decisively, even though there was a degree of risk (in relation to the possible political reaction).

> *There are times when you just have to stick your neck out, and tell the leader what you've done and why. I found evidence that a planning officer was implicated in the granting of planning permission for a small TESCO store. I set in motion an enquiry, and told the leader that's what I'd done...*

As it turned out the leader supported the chief executive's action and it helped to establish her reputation for decisiveness. But there was no guarantee that this would be the outcome.

Management Issues

Issues of this nature were identified and illustrated in Chapter 3. They reflect the understandable desire of chief executives to have a major degree of influence on personnel involved in their management teams. If chief executives are expected – as they invariably are – to establish a managerial culture that is effective in delivering the authority's priorities, then they are likely to wish to 'ease out' colleagues who are perceived as an obstacle to this goal, or in other cases, to retain colleagues who have lost favour with leading politicians. The importance for chief executives of a management team who share common values and have compatible working practices is illustrated by the following quote.

> *Soon after I was appointed, I called a Management Board meeting and made it clear that the authority was not delivering, and that we needed*

> to turn it round fast. I explained what I thought needed to be done, including a big change in the attitude to politicians. I made it clear that the approach of the previous chief executive could not continue...most of the directors did adjust, and those that didn't chose to leave....

As Chapter 3 illustrated, the nature of this type of critical incident involved a chief executive *either* standing up to a leader who wanted a chief officer (whom the chief executive valued) dismissed (although 'dismissal' as such is very difficult in a local authority – 'easing out' is a more realistic epithet) *or* convincing a leader, who was supportive of a particular chief officer, that that officer was an obstacle to the chief executive's plans, and needed to be persuaded to go. In most instances the chief executive was successful, although in the first case, the negotiation sometimes involved a period of probation, during which the chief officer was expected to prove himself or herself to the leader's satisfaction, and in the second, it sometimes took longer for the chief officer concerned to be eased out, than the chief executive would have liked. Chief executives taking charge of a 'failing authority' were typically given a more open mandate to make changes at chief officer level than those who have moved into successful (in CPA terms) authorities.

But the negotiations involved are often difficult and some interviewees felt that their authority would have been undermined, if they had not ultimately managed to achieve the outcome they wanted. One device open to chief executives, if the circumstances are propitious, is to seek to initiate a review of the management structure, as a result of which opportunities will arise to recruit a management of the chief executive's own choosing.

> *I saw one of my first challenges as changing the very traditional structures and cultures of the authority...there was 16 departments, and much policy-making was fragmented.... I managed to persuade the leadership to cut the number of departments from 16 to 5...at first, this didn't solve the problem, because the five new directorates operated very much like baronies...but over time things improved, as new appointments, which I could influence, were made.*

In this example there was a strong case for a structural reorganisation – the authority, with its 16 departments, was way out of line with comparable councils. What is much more difficult to justify, as some interviewees acknowledged, is a management restructuring the (unstated) aim of which is to make redundant an unwanted colleague.

Persuading a Reluctant Leader

This category of 'critical incident' involves situations where a chief executive is clear that a particular decision should be made, or course of action embarked upon, to which the leader is initially resistant. Alternatively, it may involve seeking to dissuade a leader from doing something which the chief executive feels should not be done. In both cases the basis of the chief executive's intervention is typically some sense of 'what is good for the authority' or for the people within it. There are circumstances when this argument can be made with reference to relatively tangible criteria, for example 'we would be likely to be legally challenged', 'this would adversely affect our CPA result' or 'we just can't afford it'. In other cases, however, the criteria involve a subjective view on the part of the chief executive about the possible impact of a decision. Here the chief executive is a difficult territory, placing his or her view of the 'good of the area' against the political judgement of a leader with a local democratic mandate.

The issues over which the chief executive seeks to persuade the leader to take a particular course of action are varied. In some cases it is a development opportunity – for example, the 'eco town' which a chief executive sought (unsuccessfully) to persuade his leader should be followed up (see Chapter 7, p. 90). Sometimes it is an issue of commitment to partnership working.

> *We had been put under pressure by the DCLG to form some kind of federation of councils (in this metropolitan area)...our leadership tended to emphasise the voluntary nature of the arrangements.... I had to tell them, no, you have to take it seriously, it's in effect a 'requirement'.*

Sometimes the issue is one of timing, for example in relation to the move to executive government in a previously '4th option' authority.

> *There was a major hiccup when the leadership decided they wanted to delay the introduction of cabinet government for another year. I managed to persuade them not to – it would have been a major setback (in CPA terms) if there had been a delay.*

Other examples from the earlier JRF research (2005) illustrate the importance of timing in seeking to persuade political leaders to face up to unwelcome decisions (e.g. the move to cabinet government).

Sometimes the challenge for a chief executive is not so much to persuade a sceptical leader, but to stiffen his or her resolve when an agreed policy generates an adverse public reaction, as in the example (see Chapter 4, p. 60) where a chief executive had to persuade a leader not to reverse a decision to close a failing school.

Other examples of chief executives pressurising reluctant leaders, discussed in earlier chapters, include exhortations in a no overall control situation that they must agree some form of administration (see Chapter 6, p. 77), or that they must take a more responsible approach to the budget (see Chapter 6, p. 79).

In another case, the chief executive recognised the opportunity provided by an impending CPA visit to argue for major changes of structure and culture, which were not at first favoured by the leadership.

> *I told them that if we behaved like this, the Audit Commission will be very critical ... we had to convince the Commission of the seriousness of our intentions (to make the necessary changes) ... the leadership was convinced by my arguments, and gave me the go ahead to do what was needed at the managerial level ...*

More problematical, perhaps, is the challenge of persuading a leader not to do something he or she is strongly predisposed to do. Sometimes the concern is about 'proprietary' issues, sometimes about processes, and sometimes about the adverse effect (in the chief executive's view) on the well-being to the area.

The incident where a chief executive felt it necessary to strongly advise a leader to distance himself from the letting of a contract in his ward has already been noted (see Chapter 7, p. 91). In another case, the problem was not one of possible impropriety but rather than what a leader wished to do was not 'covered by policy' (a crucial consideration for this chief executive, although one suspects not all). Her response was to seek an alternative way of responding to the leader's wishes, an outcome which was in due course successfully achieved.

One chief executive sought to persuade an initially unsympathetic leader in authority on the right way to deal with a politically contentious issue – the quality of elderly persons accommodation in the authority.

> *I alerted the leader to the problem, as part of our 'no surprises' agreement. His view was that we should keep the issue under wraps. I disagreed and argued that we should refer it to overview and scrutiny, so that we can show that we are being open about it and are actually dealing with the problem.*

In this case, the chief executive managed to persuade the leader to change his mind. In another 'process' issue, however the chief executive concerned was less successful.

> *I became aware that a Conservative backbencher was intending to move a 'notice of motion' at the next council meeting which I knew would get an angry response from the opposition, and wouldn't do the Conservative groups reputation – or that of the council – any good at all. The leader was away, so I had a word with his deputy, explaining why I though the motion should be withdrawn. He promised to instruct the councillor involved to do so, but on the day of the meeting, the motion was moved in its original form. The Labour group walked out...*

This intervention could be seen as an example of an unjustifiable intrusion by the chief executive into the domain of party politics. But he would see it as an attempt to safeguard the reputation (or public image) of the council. There is sometimes a fine line between these two different interpretations.

The issue of the leader with a determination to reverse the town centre policy in a way which was (in the chief executive's view) detrimental to the future of the town (see Chapter 6, p. 80) is the best example I encountered of a chief executive taking a moral stand – 'what you intend to do is perfectly legal but it is not good for the town'. Arguably it is not unreasonable for chief executives to express such views, when they feel strongly about them. The real issue is how far they are prepared to persevere with them.

Dealing with Inappropriate or Challenging Behaviour from a Leader

There is an important distinction between 'challenging' and 'inappropriate'. The chief executive who was challenged by a Liberal Democrat group leader, confident of victory in the forthcoming election, to make a case as to why the leader should trust him, (see Chapter 5, p. 65) felt it was a perfectly reasonable stance for the leader to take, and was successful in responding to the challenge.

However, this case was the exception amongst the range of behavioural examples cited, the vast majority of which related to 'inappropriate behaviour'. Within this latter category, there is a distinction between leaders who took inappropriate action (e.g. the leader who made a public commitment on library closures which breached existing policy – see Chapter 7, p. 89) and leaders who behaved to chief executives (or their management colleagues) in an inappropriate way (e.g. the chief executive who was branded as a liar in a public setting, by a leader). The second category of 'inappropriate behaviour' predominated.

Several examples of such behaviour were discussed in Chapter 4 (readers may refer if they wish to refresh their memory). Behaviour such as that of a newly elected leader who pointed at the chief executive on election night and said 'right – in my office 9.00 tomorrow' (see Chapter 5, p. 68) sets an unfortunate precedent. In this case, as in the majority of others cited, the chief executive managed to overcome this unpromising start and forged a positive relationship with the leader concerned, although the achievement of this outcome sometimes took the best part of a year. In the one or two cases where this outcome could not be achieved, the chief executive had little alternative but to seek employment elsewhere.

A different type of inappropriate behaviour was cited in relation to CPA (or service-specific) inspections. The normal practice on such occasions is for a united front, where leading members and officers in effect agree a script beforehand (indeed 'rehearsals' are by no means uncommon). Sometimes, however, the 'united front' outcome is not realised, and members say things which are likely to jeopardise the authority's rating. Two illustrative examples are provided below.

> There was a problem on the second CPA visit in 2006. The Labour leaders tried to discredit the new Lib Dem – led administration and argued that performance had declined under the new regime, I did my best to draw the inspectors attention to evidence which showed that Labour's arguments were unsound.

> Two weeks after the Conservatives gained power there was an Adult Social Services inspection. The new leader told the inspectors that the service was useless, and that this was the fault of the previous administration and the officers. As a result we got a 0 star rating for adult social services and then weak for CPA a year later because of that. I said privately to the leader 'this will come back to haunt you'.

One of the problems for chief executives in politically volatile and polarised authorities is the difficulty of persuading leaders to operate on a collective basis when faced with outside inspections. The temptation to score political points is understandable and sometimes proves too great, although the damage to the authority's rating (in CPA terms) may be significant.

There were two instances cited by chief executives who had tried to persuade a political leader not to make a particular appointment to the chair of a partnership.

> In 2004 the executive member for Children's Services decided she wanted to become a member of the Children's Trust which was overseeing the integration of children's services in the authority. There was no problem about that, but there was about the fact that she wanted to become the chair. The role of chair required a level of managerial expertise which she just didn't have. I managed to persuade the leader and her that it wouldn't be appropriate...

> When the Children's Trust was established the cabinet member for Children's services wanted to chair it. He just wasn't the right person for the job. He was very sceptical about partnership working generally, and the Trust needed an independent chair. An additional problem was that he was married to the deputy leader of the council, who kept ringing me to ask me to change my mind. I asked the leader to act as a broker,

> which he agreed... but the outcome was that the cabinet member was appointed the Chair of the Trust...

'Was this a resigning issue'? I asked the chief executive concerned. 'Not quite' was the answer, although if he had proved a totally inadequate chair, it might have become one (in fact he operated relatively competently).

Coping with Difficult Political Circumstances

The examples set out above of problematical CPA visits are also a reflection of another source of critical incidents. In a hostile political culture, a chief executive has to tread particularly carefully, as the chief executive who provided a confidential briefing to the Labour opposition, only to find it explicitly referred to at a council meeting, found out! A chief executive who had sought to support a new leader against the hostility of his predecessor (including attempts to undermine him in public) was understandably apprehensive when the former leader regained her position.[3]

> After a certain amount of finger pointing and a warning that 'things are going to change around here', we managed to resume the good working relationship that operated during her first spell as leader.

All chief executives, however experienced and competent, are prone to occasional misjudgement which, in certain circumstances, may prove a real threat to the quality of the relationship with the leader. One chief executive was commendably frank about one such misjudgement.

> Three days after the 2006 election, which the Lib Dems won, I gave an interview to a journalist from the local paper. With the benefit of hindsight, it was an error of judgement. I said that I was confident I could work with the new leader, but the way it was written up, it implied that I preferred to work with the Lib Dems rather than the Conservatives... the Conservative leader raised it the next day... 'nice picture in the paper, but I'm not happy about the content of the article'. It soon became clear that it was a big issue within the Conservative group, who felt it breached the 'political neutrality' chief executives are supposed to

> *demonstrate.... I drafted a letter to the paper concerned, discussed it with the Conservative leadership, and sent it. What I said to them was 'I know I've made a mistake – what do you want me to do put it right', which proved in the end acceptable.*

This was an authority where there was a strong possibility of the Conservatives winning the next local election. Had the matter not been resolved, it would, in this eventuality, have been difficult for the chief executive to continue in post.

Another chief executive decided to operate a 'high risk' strategy as a way of overcoming the recent history in the authority of mutual member-officer mistrust.

> *I decided to hold a workshop in informal surroundings to try to develop an improved relationship. It wasn't at all easy. Some of 'post its' at the diagnosis stage had things like 'what should members do – listen to our advice and then take it'. 'What should officers do-what we tell them' written on them... but I managed to convince them that there was an area of common ground, around the idea of delivering good services for local people. Once this common ground had been recognised it became feasible to develop mutually-acceptable ways of delivering this outcome...*

The strategy was successful, but it was a high-risk one, and one can imagine the problems the chief executive would have had in establishing credibility if the workshop had been a fiasco, as might well have happened.

Being the bearer of bad news

The final category of 'critical incidents' stems from the fact that chief executives will from time to time have to operate as the bearer of bad news – a poor CPA result, a social services overspend, a failed bid for a government-sponsored regeneration programme or a child abuse case certain to hit the national headlines. A chief executive, whose relationship with the leader is well-established and based on mutual regard, will not be likely to be blamed for the bad news; but a chief executive with a more problematical relationship with a leader may be blamed. There were several examples of chief executives having to pass on bad news, for example a discovery that the pension scheme of the council had been operating was probably illegal and potentially very costly, and a notification from a PCT that it was unable to pay a council a £4 million contribution to a joint scheme, which it had paid previously without difficulty.

CPA results are a particular minefield for leader/chief executive relationships. There may be a tendency for leaders to hold the chief executive responsible (whilst the alternative direction of blame is not feasible, except in private). There have been several examples of chief executives resigning in the aftermath of a weak or poor CPA result. None of those interviewed had suffered this indignity, although one felt he had come close to it.

> *There was a problem with the most recent CPA inspection. Adult Care Services had 'dropped a star – the Director hadn't alerted us to the problems, which meant that our overall CPA rating also dropped a category. I did wonder whether my position might be vulnerable, but fortunately the CPA report drew attention to our sound corporate management processes and arrangements.*

In this chapter the different types of 'critical incident' which can provide real tests of the strength and durability of leader/chief executive relationships have been discussed. These are the kinds of 'bottom-line' issues which can lead to a chief executive choosing to leave an authority – either because he or she does not wish to continue or because there is strong pressure from the leadership to do so. Of the chief executives interviewed only one decided that, as a result of a leader continually giving assurances and then not implementing them, he had no choice but to leave. One or two others 'considered their position' but chose to stay. In one case the trigger for a move was not a critical incident per se but a growing disillusionment with the political inertia of a long-term one-party role, after an early period of innovation and change. There are many different reasons why a chief executive chooses to step down or seek a post elsewhere. A falling-out over a critical incident which cannot be resolved satisfactorily is one important type of reason.

9
Moving On: By Choice or Otherwise

Just as decisions about which jobs to apply for (and whether or not to accept them if offered) are crucial ones for chief executives in the context of their long-term career aspirations, so are decisions about when to seek to leave existing posts and apply for new jobs, either in other local authorities or (more rarely) in other public sector organisations.

As discussed briefly in Chapter 1, there are various reasons why chief executives might wish to move on from the council in which they currently work. Two different types of motivations can be identified from the interview evidence (and a reading of relevant news items in the *MJ* and *LGC*).

- *Pull factors* reflecting genuine 'career advancement' moves
- *Push factors* reflecting a sense of dissatisfaction about some aspect of his or her job and/or the way of working in the authority (typically involving problems with the leader or the majority group).

'Pull' Factors

Ambitious chief executives may feel that a move would be beneficial in career terms, even in situations where they find an existing job fulfilling, and the relationship with the leader a positive one. There is a recognised career progression from shire district to unitary authority (or shire county) and from smaller (in population terms) examples of each genre to larger ones. In some cases there is a desire to experience working in a different kind of authority, even where there is no sense of the new job being of enhanced status. The chief executive (see Chapter 2, p. 26 above) who chose to move from a rural shire county to a deprived MB in the north because she wanted to test her ability to work in that kind of authority is one example. Another was 'headhunted' when working in a medium-sized unitary authority by a city-based unitary and felt (at that stage in his career) that it was too good an opportunity to miss. In neither case was there any dissatisfaction with their current job: rather an opportunity arose (or was sought) in career development terms.

Other chief executives sought a move or responded to an expression of interest not because of any significant dissatisfaction with their job (or with the council leader) but rather because they felt they had done as much as they could in their current authority, and didn't feel particularly stretched by the agenda facing them. As one chief executive in the JRF research (2005) put it

> I'd been at my previous authority for 15 years. We'd just received an 'excellent' CPA result, and I couldn't see what more I could do there. So when I was approached informally (by an adjacent authority) I said I'd be interested.

Another chief executive interviewed in the same research had been chief executive for an officer-led county council for several years, and welcomed an opportunity to test whether he could manage effectively in a larger county council with a more proactive political leadership.

These kinds of career moves or attempts to secure them would be widely regarded as legitimate by political leaders, however disappointed they might be at the prospect of losing a valued employee. The only problem for chief executives in such circumstances is that if it becomes known that they are looking for jobs elsewhere, this may have an impact on the quality of their relationship with their existing leader. As one interviewee put it.

> *'Fixed term contracts' would overcome the problem of applying for other jobs when you are in post, when now there are dangers of being seen as 'disloyal' by the political leadership.*

'Push' Factors

Of greater interest to an understanding of chief executive/leader relationships are reasons for moving on which reflect problems in the relationship with politicians (in particular council leaders). Two variants of problems of this nature may be distinguished; situations where a leader (or leadership group) has lost confidence in (or is increasingly unsure about) a chief executive; and situations where it is the chief executive who is increasingly unhappy about some aspect of the political culture of the authority, which may be epitomised by a particular political action or incident. In the first situation, the chief executive may wish to stay but may come to feel that his or her position is increasingly untenable. In the second they will themselves be taking the initiative to develop exit strategies.

In both cases, the perceived 'need to move on' may create real personal problems for a chief executive. Proactive career advancement moves can be sought with an awareness and acceptance of their potential impact on family life. Moves 'of necessity' may be much more difficult. Children may be at crucial stage in their education. Partners may have rewarding jobs in or close to the local authority area. In such circumstances it is not at all surprising that chief executives should do all they can to facilitate a 'tolerable' way of working with political leaders (or to 'mark time' in the hope of a (reasonably proximate) change in political control before giving up the struggle).

Some examples of the kind of political circumstances which generate a predisposition to move on the part of the chief executive have been used in Chapter 7 to illustrate the differences between 'good' and 'bad' chief executive/leader relationships. In this chapter, the opportunity has been taken to reflect not just on the interviews, but also on some of the high-profile disintegrations of chief executive/leader relationships as reported in the local government press[1], which throw a good deal of light on why chief executives sometimes feel obliged to move (rather than seek to do so for more positive reasons).

In what circumstances might a political leader lose confidence in a chief executive? The following possibilities can be identified.

- Situations where a chief executive is held responsible (whether fairly or unfairly) for publicised 'poor performance'.

- Situations where a chief executive has played a 'whistleblowing role' in a way which has caused embarrassment (or worse) for political leaders.
- Other aspects of a chief executive's behaviour which are deemed politically unacceptable (e.g. the premature leaking of a critical report)
- A breakdown in the personal relationship; a leader who feels he or she cannot work with particular chief executives (or, in a few cases, anticipates that they will be unable to do so).

These different circumstances may of course operate in a 'chain reaction'. An unacceptable incidence of behaviour by a chief executive may lead to a breakdown of the personal relationship with the leader. Or a problematic personal relationship may be exacerbated by a poor CPA result.

The circumstances in which chief executives might 'lose confidence' in or feel they can no longer work with political leaders are to some extent the mirror images of these situations (in particular the third and fourth) and indeed may occur in parallel (e.g. both leader and chief executive find the other's behaviour unacceptable, or both possibly for different reasons – find the relationship 'unworkable'). In two other cases, however, the situations are unique to the chief executive.

There are thus for chief executives two parallel situations with those in which leaders feel they can no longer work with chief executives.

- Chief executives may find some aspects of a leader's behaviour unacceptable (in terms of their ability to provide effective managerial leadership).
- A chief executive may find the personal relationship with a leader unworkable.

But there are also situations which do not have a parallel.

- Chief executives may seek to move in anticipation of crisis or an unwelcome change of political control or leadership.
- A chief executive may perceive his or her role and status to have been undermined, not necessarily by the leader but by some network of leading members/officers which is critical of him or her.

Leaders Losing Confidence in Chief Executives

Attributed responsibility for poor performance

Directors of Education, Social Services and (more recently) Children's Services have for the past 30 years been vulnerable to critical external assessments. OFSTED and the Social Services Inspectorate have been assessing the quality of services in these categories since the 1980s and there have been numerous examples of members responding to such reports by advising the Director concerned to seek employment elsewhere. This is not always the way the scenario develops; sometimes members are prepared to recognise that they may have contributed to the shortcomings identified in the report, and sometimes they may be confident that the Director (especially if recently appointed) has the capacity to 'turn things round'. For the Directors of Social Services and (since 2002) Children's Services there has been the added 'performance-related' hazard of the horrific headline-hitting cases of child abuse which (probably inevitability) slip through the net of the departments concerned from time to time. Again there is the temptation for members to attribute blame (as well as formal responsibility) to the Director concerned and to seek to engineer his or her departure.

The introduction of the CPA in 2002 presented, for the first time, an equivalent performance hazard for chief executives. Previously, although there were occasionally cases of authorities being castigated for being badly-run, this was very much the exception. Even if leading members or members of the public suspected that an authority was being poorly managed at the corporate level, there was no external inspection mechanism to confirm (or dispel) such impressions, until the CPA come along.

The key difference between CPA and the service inspections is that the role of politics and politicians in the performance of an authority is part of the assessment made. The damning corporate governance reports issued by the Audit Commission to authorities such as Kingston-upon-Hull (2003), Stoke-on-Trent (2003), Lincolnshire (2005) and North Tyneside (2003) made it clear that the responsibility for weak or poor performance did not lie solely with the officers (and in particular the chief executive) – the political culture had also made a significant impact, through problems such as weak leadership, involvement in micromanagement, unproductive inter-party squabbles, avoidance of 'difficult' decisions and so on. Thus it was in principle less justifiable to attribute blame wholly to the chief executive (unless he or she had been singled out in the report concerned).

However, such 'shared responsibility' verdicts have not prevented political leaders from deciding that chief executives should be held accountable. The influential SOLACE report 'Managing in Political Environment' (2006) recognises this problem.

> The pressures of outside inspection such as the CPA...a poor report may lead to speculation and unhelpful division between members and officers as to who was responsible and who should 'carry the can'. (p. 34)

The phenomenon of 'disputed responsibility' was well-illustrated by an *MJ* news item on the troubled district council of Tunbridge Wells

> Pressure for the chief executive of poorly-performing Tunbridge Wells BC to quit is mounting. Insiders told the local press that councillors at the Tory-led borough which was placed in the 'weak' category at the last CPA inspection were calling for Rodney Stone to stand down.
>
> The CPA identified lack of political and managerial leadership...at the root of poor performance.... Tunbridge Wells is said to be split apart over the chief executive's position. His supporters argue that blame for the council's troubles cannot be laid in the lap of one person, when there was strife amongst political leaders and back-bencher councillors felt disenfranchised...but others consider getting rid of the current chief a starting point for much-needed change.
>
> (*MJ* 20 January 2005)

Sometimes it is the anticipation of a poor CPA assessment which sparks off the perception that a change of chief executive is needed.

> Paul Doherty is likely to be the next chief executive to be ousted as troubles at Swindon BC reached crisis point.... Conservatives and Liberal Democrats will bond together to force his departure following damning OFSTED and Social Services reports and

the CPA inspection which is expected to be dire.... Conservative leader councillor Mike Bowden told the MJ 'we have expressed our lack of confidence in him and think someone with a fresh approach should be taking his place'.

(*MJ* 1 August 2003)

Indeed, being associated with a poor (or weak) CPA assessment and being 'replaced' as a result is a nightmare scenario for a chief executive, the chances of re-appointment to a similar post are slim indeed. Yet the potential unfairness of this kind of judgement has been recognised, not only by SOLACE.

The question is raised whether chief executives... can reasonably he held responsible for the barriers which an unstable or conflictual political climate can provide to the achievement of a good CPA rating... in my view, the CPA process should take the political culture of an authority as given and concentrate on the performance of the authority is management **in the political circumstances in which they have to operate**.

(Leach 2010, forthcoming)

Such expressions of concern will be little comfort to deposed chief executives in authorities such as Walsall, Hull or Tunbridge Wells. There were further dangers for incumbent chief executives in a CPA inspection. The team which carried out the review would typically include one or more local politicians (usually council leaders). If they were from the same party as that which formed the administration in the authority, under review there was the potential for an informal (and private) channel of discussion about the problems facing the authority including the merits or otherwise of the chief executive. The use of this informal channel appears to be at the root of pressure to remove the chief executive of LB Hillingdon in 2006.

The bitter row between the chief executive of Hillingdon LBC and council's leader has taken a new twist, after it emerged London's top council leader said the borough's chief 'should go' if 'the council was to move forward'. The Audit Commission has been forced to deny it was behind the remark after Hillingdon leader

Ray Puddifoot allegedly claimed it has passed judgement on chief executive Duncan Leatham in an official CPA inspection...the leader allegedly claimed the CPA named Mr Leatham as a 'key weak component' holding the council back, Mr Bundred insisted the inspection made 'no negative references to managerial leadership'. But he said the CPA team leader...had said a 'comment along these lines' was made by fellow team member councillor Merrick Cockell, Kensington and Chelsea RLBC, leader...during a meeting between the two leaders.

(*MJ* 19 October 2006)

Adverse reaction to chief executive as whistleblower

There are situations in which a chief executive will feel it necessary to 'report' a council leader to the Standards Board (or the District Auditor) for some form of misconduct which he or she sees as too serious to be resolved internally and informally. For chief executives who are also the council's monitoring officer, it would be their responsibility to lodge the complaint. If another officer who has this role, it would have to be done formally through them, although the leader could reasonably assume that it was the chief executive who had set the process in motion.

There is an important area of judgement here for a chief executive. If he or she makes a formal complaint of this nature it is highly unlikely that the leader and chief executive would be able to work together again, nor would either expect it. In making such a complaint, the chief executive is (in effect) terminating his working relationship with the current leader, knowing that if the complaint is not upheld (or is upheld, but not considered serious enough for the leader to resign) his or her own position would be untenable. That knowledge is bound to influence his or her judgement.

There are instances where chief executives have used their judgement and chosen not to report an errant leader. In the JRF research (2005), one chief executive told us.

> When the new leader was elected, my first task was to confront him with evidence of an (on-the-face-of-it) fraudulent expenses claim. I managed to persuade him to acknowledge that the claim was inappropriate, and that he should pay the money back, to avoid action being taken against him.

In another case, however, the chief executive decided that formal action was necessary.

> Liberal Democrat leader Chris Slyfield has resigned as leader of Waverley BC and delivered an outspoken attack on the 'climate of fear and relentless secrecy at the council'... he disclosed that the chief executive Christine Pointer had reported him to the Standards Board shortly before the 2003 elections. Miss Pointer insisted that she had acted correctly in informing the Standards Board.... 'I stand by my decision on the evidence before me in 2003. There could have been a breach of the Waverley Code of Conduct...
>
> (*MJ* 10 February 2005)

The added complication of the chief executive's action in this case was that reporting took place just before the 2003 local election, when Councillor Slyfield was the opposition leader. When he became council leader after the election, the relationship with the chief executive must have been extremely difficult for both parties.

The most celebrated recent case of whistleblowing occurred in Lincolnshire, where in 2001, the chief executive David Bowles reported the then leader Jim Speechley to the District Auditor for a variety of breaches of rules and regulations, including the Members Code of Conduct. This action set in motion a process whereby the leader was convicted in 2004 for 'misconduct in public office' (through trying to influence the route of a bypass to increase the value of land he owned) and jailed for 18 months.[2]

In an interview later in 2004, David Bowles made some pertinent observations about his relationship with the leader. The clash was not, he argued, about personality or politics, it was about abuse of power.

> Speechley was quite a forceful character, but I think you have to be able to work with all sorts of people... none of the disagreements have been strategic or political. Every chief executive may have to implement policies they wouldn't support personally. It was about abuse of power. They were issues of fiefdom and disobeying rules and regulations.
>
> (*MJ* 14 October 2004, p. 20)

These are important distinctions. David Bowles's argument was that chief executives should be able to cope with personality differences and differences of views about policies, but that evidence of misconduct has to be dealt with firmly, even if it means the breakdown of the relationship with the leader. In this case there was an added problem that the council's monitoring officer had refused to take action over the chief executive's concerns, and was subsequently suspended by him (the District Auditor's 2002 report noted 'an almost complete absence of monitoring officer intervention in any of a series of issues of concern', and was critical of his 'close relationship' with the leader and deputy).

However, the problematic nature of the leader/chief executive relationship in Lincolnshire clearly went much deeper than the misconduct issues concerned. In his evidence to the court hearing in 2004, David Bowles characterised his relationship with the leader in the following terms.

> I have had four years of dealing with a person – and I am not saying this with malice, I have tried very carefully to be fair and even-handed – I have spent four years dealing with a person who is the most deceitful and dishonest person I have ever had to work with, who has subjected me to malicious comments.
>
> (*LGC* 5 March 2004)

This characterisation sounds like the basis for an unworkable relationship, with the crucial ingredients (see Chapter 1, pp. 22–25) of mutual trust and mutual respect palpably absent.

There was a further chapter of the Lincolnshire story when Ian Croft took over the leadership of the county council following Jim Speechley's conviction. The chief executive's action had been seen to be totally justified and he might have reasonably expected to resume his post. However, this was not the outcome which occurred, following the breakdown in the relationship between the new leader and David Bowles (see Chapter 9, p. 121 below).

A second 'cause celebre' which revolved around whistleblowing became apparent in June 2004, 'Cheltenham BC's managing director Christine Laird was suspended on full pay for two months following the ongoing dispute between her and the council leader Andrew McKinley. The dispute dated from the previous summer when Ms Laird and the council's three opposition groups made a complaint about McKinley to the Standards Board' (*LGC* 10 June 2004). The added complication here is the fact that the complaint was made by the chief executive *and* the three opposition party groups. A direct alignment between chief executive and the political opponents of the leader is certainly a high-risk strategy. Ms Laird left her post in August 2005. The Cheltenham, Lincolnshire and Waverley cases all illustrate the consequences for a chief executive's tenure of office of whistleblowing (however justified it may be).

Perceived 'unacceptable behaviour' of chief executive

'Whistleblowing' is one example of what is likely to be perceived by a council leader as 'unacceptable behaviour' (whether or not the perception turns out justified). However, there are other categories of chief executive behaviour which leaders may find unacceptable and may, in certain circumstances, result in the chief executive being told they are no longer wanted.

Sometimes the perceived 'unacceptable behaviour' relates to a particular incident, sometimes to a series of incidents. A news story in the *MJ* (4 December 2003) revealed that the chief executive of LB Bromley had received a letter from the legal director which included the following.

> The leader's position is that he can no longer trust you because you have acted and will continue to act towards him and his colleagues in a way which undermines his position.

This extract implies an ongoing 'behavioural problem' (the details of the behaviour were never identified). However, in other cases, it is a specific incident which leads to a loss of confidence. Some of the critical incidents discussed in Chapter 8 provide examples of chief executive behaviour which political leaders found (at the very least) questionable. The chief executive who gave an interview to the local paper which implied a preference for working with the Liberal Democrat rather than a Conservative administration (see Chapter 8, p. 106 above) may not have survived had the Conservatives been returned to power at the next election (although in fact she managed to retrieve the situation), Lin Homer's position as chief executive of Birmingham City Council was made more difficult by the publication of a critical report on the council's handling of electoral fraud at the 2005 council elections.

> The council was criticised during the electoral fraud trial of six Labour councillors... the judge concluded there 'was evidence of fraud which would disgrace a banana republic' during last June's local elections, when Ms Homer was the returning officer... although he did not claim her conduct had been flawed, he did say the vote had not been conducted in strict adherence to electoral rules.
>
> (*MJ* 9 December 2005)

Sometimes association with, rather than direct responsibility for, 'bad news' is enough to create problems for a chief executive.

The most high-profile example of an authority where leading politicians found the behaviour of a chief executive unacceptable comes from the much-troubled Kingston-upon-Hull City Council. In April 2002, Jim Brooks was appointed chief executive of the council moving from the relative tranquillity of Poole BC. An *MJ* article 'Why I moved from haven to Hull' published a few months later was full of optimism, the chief executive having recently won all-party support for an 82-page recovery plan. 'For me, this is a three-to-five year programme', he said. 'They've hired me to transform the organisation, not to get through the CPA' (*MJ* 14 November 2002).

Ironically, it was a damning CPA report which proved an insurmountable problem. In June 2003, the new Labour administration suspended the chief executive. What the new administration found unacceptable was the fact that Mr Brooks had authorised the publication by the Liberal Democrat leadership of a draft copy of a scathing Audit Commission report.

> He claims he was given the go-ahead after discussing it with the Audit Commission, but they say they would never 'condone' the publicising of a draft report... the new council leader Colin Inglis says 'we made no complaint about the chief executive to the Standards Board, but following a year-long investigation, it has emerged that he was deeply implicated in a series of actions which led to the conclusion the Board has announced. Councillors must

be able to have confidence in the actions taken and the advice offered by the council's chief executive'.

(*MJ* 12 June 2003)

Jim Brooks' version of events is very different from the council leader's and the chief executive's union ALACE threatened to blacklist the authority's top job if the ministers did not act to deal with the situation (*MJ* 26 June 2003). In fact Jim Brooks never returned to a post he had held for just over a year. A severance package was agreed in November 2003.

The problem for the chief executive in this instance was not that of alienating the leader he was working with at the time, but of failing to predict the response of the main opposition group to his action, with a local election pending at which they had a good chance of returning to power (which is what in fact happened). In Waverley there was a similar scenario where the chief executive reported to the Standards Board an opposition leader who a short time later became council leader. In neither case is there an implication that the chief executive's actions were unjustified. Rather the conclusion to be drawn is the importance to thinking through the impact of possible changes of political control, when deciding on a controversial course of action. Political judgement is an immensely important 'requisite quality' for chief executives particularly in politically turbulent authorities such as Hull and Lincolnshire.

A breakdown in personal relationships

There is always the possibility that a leader and chief executive may experience personality clashes, even (in extremis) may actually dislike each other. This mutual dislike may be accentuated by incidents which highlight their different ways of working (e.g. a leader who treats key partners dismissively at a partnership board, at which the chief executive is seeking to build positive relationships). But such incidents are not a necessary ingredient of a dysfunctional relationship, which may develop simply if the two individuals concerned have very different (and incompatible) personal styles.

The long-running Lincolnshire saga provides a further example of a breakdown of personal relations. David Bowles, whose stand against Jim Speechley was vindicated by the report of the District Auditor, and later by the conviction of the leader for misconduct in public office, could reasonably have expected to retain his position as chief executive. However, Ian Croft who replaced Jim Speechley as leader had other ideas.

> Despite the conviction, Conservative leader Ian Croft, a long-time friend of Speechley is determined to prevent Mr Bowles returning to work from sick leave. Mr Bowles wants to return, but solicitors acting for the council leadership have told him not to, in a letter with the word 'not' emphasised in capital letters... in a radio interview Mr Croft was asked whether the chief executive should quit. He responded if you're asking me to speculate – then I think the answer is yes.

The situation here was that a new leader, indignant at the chief executive's role in exposing the former leader's misconduct, felt that a relationship between himself and the chief executive would be unworkable. In effect the relationship had 'broken down' before it began to operate, on the basis of the attitude and expectation of the new leader. In the event David Bowles sought (and received) a substantial settlement from the county and did not return. Ian Croft (and all his cabinet colleagues) resigned in March 2005 following a further damning 'corporate governance' inspection report from the Audit Commission. In April 2006 he was barred from holding political office for 15 months for 'abusing his powers to undermine the council's "exemplary" chief executive'.

In this example, as in many other struggling leader/chief executive relationships, the lack of trust is often a major factor. Although it is possible that two individuals who dislike each other may nonetheless trust each other, it is much less likely that 'mutual trust' will exist, than if the two individuals enjoyed a good personal relationship. It has been argued earlier that mutual trust (and indeed mutual respect) does not guarantee an effective leader/chief executive relationship; one must also take into account the need for an appropriate division of responsibilities and for workable conflict resolution mechanisms. But in the absence of mutual trust, it is difficult to see how a relationship can be sustained beyond the short term.

When chief executives find it impossible to work with leaders

Unacceptable behaviour of leader and relationship breakdown

In major disputes between a chief executive and council leader, whilst (as we have seen) a leader may find a chief executive's behaviour unacceptable (e.g. the new (Labour) leader's view of Jim Brooks's release of the draft CPA report in 2003), so may chief executives find a leader's behaviour unacceptable. However, it is not uncommon for ad hoc 'unacceptable behaviour' on the leader's part to occur from time to time, and for this to be accepted as part of the job (see Chapter 8). It usually only becomes a reason for moving on when it is persistent, systematic and revolves round 'bottom line' issues, typically concerning the division of responsibilities.

Indeed there were some examples from the research of chief executives putting up with 'unacceptable' behaviour of this nature for a relatively long period of time. One female chief executive I interviewed had experienced real difficulties with a pompous, inflexible and (to a degree) sexist male leader with a tendency to bully her (and indeed other chief officers, party colleagues and opposition councillors). The post was her first appointment and she found ways of dealing with the leader that made the relationship just about tolerable. But there was great relief when the leader lost power at an election and was replaced by a more reasonable individual.

In Chapter 7 the difficulties experienced by a chief executive who found a particular leader unreliable and untrustworthy were discussed. The chief executive's impending departure (by choice) was stalled when there was a change of administration and the leaders of the new coalition offered him incentives to stay. Two years later however, the coalition lost power, the former leader returned, and the chief executive decided that he did not want to continue.

However, persistent unacceptable behaviour of this nature is more likely to lead to a chief executive seeking to move on (typically having negotiated a substantial severance package). For example in Chapter 7, the case was discussed of a chief executive who made a series of attempts to resolve a problematic relationship with the leader who had appointed him, but in the end despaired of the leader's ability to keep his word and decided he could not continue in the post.

In this section the two motivations for departure – 'unacceptable leader behaviour' and 'breakdown of the relationship' – are discussed together. Unacceptable behaviour often leads to relationship breakdown; or alternatively the breakdown of the relationship may spark off (further) incidences of the unacceptable behaviour. The two phenomena are typically inextricably intertwined.

It should also be emphasised that there is usually (though not always) a similar symbiotic relationship between perceived unacceptable behaviour on a leader's part and on a chief executive's part. Whilst Jim Speehley clearly found David Bowles's behaviour unacceptable, the chief executive had the same view of the leader's behaviour. The same point applies to Colin Inglis and Jim Brooks in Kingston-upon-Hull, and in Cheltenham, North East Derbyshire, Hillingdon and elsewhere.

The dispute between Liverpool's chief executive David Henshaw and the Liberal Democrat leadership of Liverpool City Council in the 2005–2006 period provides an example of a series of 'unacceptable' political behaviours ultimately motivating David Henshaw to seek other positions. The dispute first hit the headlines in March 2005 'Henshaw quits Liverpool' (*MJ* 24 March 2005), although the message involved in the headline turned out to be premature. Sir David Henshaw did not, in the event, quit until early 2006. The first manifestation of the dispute was over his pension.

> Liverpool City Council chief Sir David Henshaw has announced that he will quit after a wrangle with councillors over his pension. The council refused to compensate Sir David to the tune of £200,000 after he realised he would lose out under changes to pension rules.... Liverpool leader Mike Storey said 'We have decided not to go down the route of enhancing the chief executive's pension. I could not support treating one person differently from everyone else'.
>
> (*MJ* 24 March 2005)

A month later, however, the headline in the same journal read 'Henshaw stays' and noted that Sir David has said he hopes to stay on, after an unprecedented statement of support from Councillor Mike Storey who vowed 'I will do everything I can to make sure he stays' (*MJ* 28 April 2005). Including compensation over loss of pension presumably? However, a year later it became apparent that the dispute over Sir David's pension had not been a 'one-off' problem. There were it appeared more systematic problems in the leader/chief executive relationship.

> Liverpool City Council leader Mike Storey and chief executive Sir David Henshaw have hit the headlines again – this time over a report that chronicles a major breakdown in their working relationship. The section 151 report by executive director says an investigation of e-mails and mobile phone records shows 'evidence of a clear conspiracy' between Councillor Storey and the suspended head of media Matt Finnegan to force Sir David out of his position as chief executive ... it also recommends that a copy of the full report, with copies of e-mail messages and mobile phone records ... should be sent to the Standards Board.
> (*MJ* 26 May 2005)

Although there was in October 2005 an agreement between leader and chief executive to 'bury the hatchet, after their relationship approached breaking point' (*MJ* 20 October 2005) this was swiftly overtaken by further revelations regarding the 'conduct of Sir David and resources director Phil Halsall, over a set of private e-mails which become public knowledge' (ibid). In December 2005, councillor Mike Storey resigned after 'an error of judgement' breached the code of conduct and brought his authority into disrepute' (*MJ* 1 December 2005). His successor as leader Councillor Warren Bradley then refused to give his backing to the chief executive.

> The new leader remained silent over the details of the dispute (between Councillor Storey and Sir David Henshaw) but did admit it was difficult to commit to what his working relationship with Sir David would be....' I will be building a new team and if David Henshaw wants to be part of the team, I will be happy for that to happen. But I wouldn't like to say yes or no at this stage as to whether we'll be able to form a good working relationship.
> (*MJ* 8 December 2005)

In the light of this equivocation, it is not surprising that in 2006, Sir David Henshaw decided to seek posts elsewhere.[3] This sequence of events provides a number of insights into how leader/chief executive relationships can deteriorate and then have knock-on effects if a leader resigns or is barred from office. First the pension dispute in 2005 clearly proved a destabilising event in the relationship. There are likely to have been prior tensions in the relationship, but the leader's negative response to the chief executive's request appears to have moved the relationship further into conflict mode (despite the apparent reconciliations a month later). The exchange of e-mails between the leader and the head of media took place only a few months after the pension incident. Secondly there was a sense of 'cumulative breakdown'. Once the relationship had been destabilised it went from bad to worse. There may have been a degree of mutual respect and mutual trust before March 2005, but these qualities were clearly absent subsequently. Thirdly, as in the Lincolnshire case (see Chapter 9, p. 117–119 above) problems may not be over when a problematic leader (from the chief executive's perspective) resigns. If his or her successor holds the view that the chief executive has contributed to a valued colleague's displacement, there is likely to be an antipathy to working with that chief executive. That was clearly the case in Lincolnshire when Paul Croft took over from Jim Speechley. It was also apparent when Warren Bradley took over from Mike Storey in Liverpool. Fourthly the perils of the use of e-mails to pass on sensitive information or to express controversial views are to be noted. They clearly played a key role in the aggravation of the dispute in Liverpool, as they did also in Cheltenham (see Chapter 9, p. 119 above).

Undermining of chief executive's role by councillor/officer network

In the absence of a dysfunctional relationship with the leader, a chief executive may still feel it difficult to continue, if there are informal channels operating between other chief officers and cabinet members which bypass him or her, and may in certain circumstances be seeking to undermine his or her authority. This was certainly a problem for one of the chief executives interviewed.

> In 2006 there was a big increase in the size of the Conservative group, and the leader's position appears to have been weakened.... I can no

longer get access to the whole group in the way I could in 2003. Also members are spending a lot of time listening to staff criticism about the way the authority is being managed .... I don't think this is appropriate, but I'm not clear what I can do about it.

At least this chief executive had retained the confidence and support of his leader. In situations where the leader (or his or her closest allies) is using informal channels with other chief officers in ways which undermine the chief executive's authority, then the chief executive's position becomes increasingly vulnerable. An informal channel of communication between the leader and the head of media was clearly used in this way in Liverpool (see above). There was a similar link between Jim Speechley and the monitoring officer on Lincs CC. A parallel problem faced another chief executive.

There is a ruling mafia behind the leadership group which works with a wider set of allies, some of them in key positions in the council. One director I know has a 'direct line' to the leader. So does the head of communications. It got to the stage where I couldn't even trust my own management team.

The ideal situation for a chief executive is one where there is a strong leader (strong in the sense of being able to get his or her own way in cabinet and party group meetings) with whom the chief executive has a positive, trustful relationship. If there is an added ingredient of a management team the chief executive can trust (and possibly dominate) then his or her position is secure indeed. Remove any of these ingredients – resulting in any or all of a mistrustful leader; an ineffective leader; a disunited management team and powerful member officer alliance which bypass the chief executive – and it is well nigh impossible for him or her to manage the authority effectively.

Anticipation of crises or political change

One of the reasons why chief executives begin to study the local government vacancies pages of the *Guardian* with an increasing sense of urgency may be a sense of impending crisis, which may be in the form of externally generated 'bad news' – a poor or weak CPA result – or a likely change of leadership or political control with which the chief executive does not want to have to deal. The metaphor 'jumping before you are pushed' is pertinent in this connection. One reported incidence of this nature was as follows.

> Joyce Markham has denied rumours that she has applied for the vacant chief executive post at Warwickshire CC, in an effort to leave Harrow LBC. The London borough has been awash with rumours that Ms Markham was looking for a new job, following the controversial sacking of executive director Tony Lear. One insider claimed it was well known she was going for other jobs, a charge the chief executive denied... (her denial) contradicts speculation that Ms Markham is trying to jump before she is pushed, and as a result of the fallout from the sacking of Mr Lear.
> (*MJ* 16 June 2005)

Whatever the truth of the matter, this cameo well illustrates this kind of situation where it might be understandable for a chief executive to seek to jump before being pushed.

Another chief executive began to look around for other jobs in the face of a likely change of control at the next election and the possibility of a particular individual to whom she had a strong personal antipathy (see Chapter 5, p. 68 above).

Other chief executives with similar apprehensions have chosen to stay and see how it works out. In reality, the possibility of unwelcome political change is unlikely to be a sufficient reason for contemplating a move. It is more likely to be an additional influence on the decision of a chief executive who feels ready for a new challenge anyway.

Conclusion

In this chapter we have discussed situations in which chief executives may feel it appropriate to seek jobs elsewhere. If they are doing so for career advancement reasons, the process is relatively uncontentious, unless a scenario develops in which chief executives move frequently – every 2 years or so – for career advancement purposes, in which case there is an argument that they would be likely to leave behind a trail of 'unfinished business'. If, however, their desire to move is the result of a breakdown of their relationship with the council leader, the process is much more likely to be contentious (and more likely to hit the front pages of the *MJ* and *LGC*).

The emphasis in this chapter has been on such contentious 'reasons for departure', because such cases can tell us a great deal about the potential weak points and stumbling blocks in chief executive/leader relationships. However, these high-profile cases should be seen in context. Most chief executives do not leave councils because they have fallen out with council leaders. The more usual pattern is for them to move elsewhere for career advancement reasons, or to retire when they feel ready to do so.

If the relationship with the leader has irretrievably broken down, three strategies are open to a chief executive; first to 'jump before you are pushed' (particularly pertinent to the impending crisis/change of political control); secondly to seek to negotiate a financial settlement prior to seeking a new job elsewhere; and third to 'stick it out' in the hope that the unacceptable aspects of the political context will dissipate. The second and third options can be pursued in the knowledge that it is in fact very difficult for leading members to 'dismiss' a chief executive, unless there is clear evidence of misconduct on his or her part. Leading members know that if this evidence is not conclusive, chief executives will be well-supported at any hearing by the SOLACE network, which can draw on individuals well-skilled at fighting cases of this nature. The only other option is to engineer a restructuring which makes the chief executive's position 'surplus to requirements' (typically by substituting a lower profile 'managing director' role or introducing a collective managerial leadership – see Chapter 12 for further discussion). However, this process takes time and is also open to challenges, particularly if the structural review is carried out internally (by someone other than the chief executive!). If neither of these two options are seen as feasible, political leaders are left with the option of making life as unpleasant as possible for the incumbent chief executive (or, of course, seeking to rehabilitate the relationship).

10
The Impact of Inspection and the Performance Culture

There have been two major legislative changes which have impacted upon relationships between chief executives and council leaders since 2000. The first was the introduction in 2001 of local executive government (whether mayoral or – much more commonly – non-mayoral). The second was the increasingly interventionist inspectorial role of the Audit Commission, in particular the impact of the CPA (Comprehensive Performance Assessment) system introduced in 2002.[1] The first change has subsequently been given further momentum by the provisions of the 2007 Local Government Act, which strengthen the position of council leaders (in particular their 4-year security of tenure). It has had less impact on the relationship than might have been anticipated, for reasons which are discussed in Chapter 11. The second change has had a more profound effect, for reasons which are discussed below.

Local authorities have long been accustomed to assessments of their performance – typically through inspection – of the individual services for which they are responsible. OFSTED inspections of education authorities and the work of the Social Service Inspectorate were well-established before Labour came to power in 1997. The introduction of the 'Best Value' concept in its first period of office led to a further range of inspections and assessments.

The political dimension of the CPA

What was unprecedented about the introduction of the CPA system from 2002 onwards was that it sought to provide an *overall* measure of the performance of all local authorities, by combining (in a far from transparent formula) individual *service-specific* assessments with a *corporate* assessment which endeavoured to rate and classify the political/managerial competence of the authority. As a result of this process, authorities were classified as excellent, good, fair, weak or poor. Since 2006, this categorisation has been replaced by a star system (0–4) combined with an assessment of the extent of (and capacity for) improvement.

Whereas the move to cabinet government at the local level involved a potential switch of power from officers to councillors (although this potential was by no means always realised), the introduction of the CPA had an impact in the reverse direction. Just as a headteacher's career can be boosted by a good OFSTED report or adversely affected by a poor one, so chief executives' reputations are substantially affected by a CPA rating. Although councillors will typically be pleased about a good/excellent result and concerned about a weak/poor one, it has a less direct impact on their political careers, particularly when it became apparent that CPA score had little discernable impact on subsequent local electoral outcomes. However, a weak or poor inspection result will sometimes lead to a search for scapegoats (see below), a process which may jeopardise a chief executive's job security.

As the CPA is primarily a mechanism for managerial assessment, it is the chief executive who will inevitably 'lead' the process of establishing a way of working which seeks to convince the CPA that the authority should be rated as 'excellent' or 'good'. Of course, the responsibility for performance in relation to education, social services and other commonly-assessed services (such as housing benefits) will rest primarily with the service directors concerned, although the chief executive will want to do all he or she can to facilitate good performance in these services (not least by seeking to influence appointment processes, so that applicants who are seen as potential 'good performers' are selected). But certainly in relation to the corporate assessment – an absolutely crucial element in the CPA process – chief executives will see themselves as having primary responsibility for delivering a good/excellent rating.

The problem for a chief executive is that establishing the ingredients that would be likely to lead to a good corporate assessment requires co-operation from the leading councillors. An analysis of

CPA reports, which I carried out in 2005–2006, demonstrates clearly that there was within the CPA process a view of how politics should operate. It was also apparent that some of the qualities which a good corporate assessment would be expected to demonstrate would only be possible if politicians were, in many cases, prepared to change their attitude to issues such as strategy, partnership and public involvement.

The analysis noted above (see Leach 2010) identified a series of 'expectations' surrounding the Audit Commission's assessment procedures. In management terms, an authority which hoped to receive a good assessment had to demonstrate that it has all or most of the following qualities:

- A clear set of priorities (which incorporate priorities expected by central government) drawn together into a coherent corporate strategy
- which operates in conjunction with a well-designed performance management system
- a positive attitude to partnership working which provides a 'joined-up' approach to the issues which require them
- a readiness to consult the public and reflect public priorities in the council's strategy
- a clear division of labour between officers and councillors which (inter alia) minimises the involvement of the latter in day-to-day decision-making.

In conjunction with these requirements (and drawing on my analysis of CPA reports) there is a distinction which can be drawn between a 'good political authority' and a 'poor' one.

The 'Good' political authority

The good political authority is one in which there is strong but inclusive political leadership, preferably with a degree of continuity. The dominant party (or coalition) seeks consensus between all parties on priorities which are 'for the good of the area', but encourages challenge from non-executive members, particularly through the scrutiny system. Members concentrate on strategic issues and delegate all operational decisions to managers; however, they maintain a lively involvement in performance management. They take a proactive and positive view of partnership working. Decision-making processes are characterised by speediness, readiness to confront 'difficult' decisions, responsiveness to public opinion and a readiness to communicate openly 'bad news' as well as 'good news'.

The 'poor' political authority

The poor political authority is in many ways the antithesis of the 'good'. It is one in which there is weak leadership, and a conflictual inter-party climate, with a vulnerability to regular changes in political control. The dominant party attempts to minimise the capacity of the opposition to challenge its performance in a constructive way. Members have a tendency to parochialism and involve themselves in operational issues. They exhibit a tendency to evade or delay difficult decisions and publicise 'good news' whilst hiding 'bad news'. They display little in the way of a coherent political strategy and little in the way of a coherent approach to performance management. They are unenthusiastic about partnership working. Party priorities prevail over the priorities of the local community.

It can be argued that in developing and applying these different models in what is basically a managerial evaluation, the Audit Commission is inappropriately involving itself in political territory which should be outside its remit. It is also the case that its' view of the role of party politics is somewhat unrealistic and unnecessarily prescriptive. However, chief executives know that (in relation to the CPA) the Audit Commission's view of politics matters.

Chief Executives and the CPA

In circumstances where the political leader is prepared to operate supportively (and can carry his or her political group with him), it is likely that the chief executive's views about what needs to be done to achieve ideas for achieving a good/excellent CPA outcome will be taken forward. But what if support of this nature is not forthcoming?

The problem for chief executives is that they may be held responsible (by the Audit Commission and by leading politicians) for the barriers which an unstable or conflictual political climate can provide to the achievement of some of the characteristics required for a good (or satisfactory) CPA rating. There is certainly evidence from my recent research that chief executives have in these circumstances sought to:

- persuade councillors that they should develop and own a corporate strategy which embodies a limited set of clear priorities
- include in the strategy certain items which reflect central government priorities which are not necessarily shared by the dominant group
- commission and take account of surveys of public opinion in deciding priorities
- take a more proactive and inclusive approach to partnership working
- modify overview and scrutiny arrangements to involve a sharing of chairs and the facilitation of a greater degree of challenge.

Whilst some administrations may be responsive to some or all of these attempts at influence from chief executives, others will resist them often for perfectly justifiable political reasons. If this proves to be the case, it will emerge at the visit of the CPA team, as well as in their observation of meetings and analysis of documentation. And whatever the reality of the responsibility for a weak or poor CPA result, a poor report as the 2005 SOLACE report points out 'may lead to speculation and unhelpful divisions between members and officers as to who should "carry the can" ' (SOLACE (2006, p. 57)).

The point to emphasise is that the advent of an inspectoral regime like the CPA, in which an authority is classified in relation to political/managerial qualities, which a chief executive can deliver only with the co-operation and support of the political administration, has proved an important new influence on the relationship and resulted in new pressures on chief executives to influence political leaders.

In these circumstances, it is not surprising that the chief executives interviewed often had a good deal to say about the importance of CPA, and the efforts they had made to ensure a good (or ideally excellent) result. In some cases, chief executives were appointed to improve CPA performance in authorities which had either been classified as weak or poor, or anticipated an outcome of this nature.

> At the time of my appointment, it was clear that the council was heading for at best a 'weak' CPA result. One of the reasons I was appointed was members' expectation that I could turn the authority round. They were looking for a lead... which gave me a good deal of scope to introduce change.

Another chief executive reported a similar expectation, of 'turning the authority round', although 'there was no clear idea from members as to what this might involve'.

Where leading members are particularly keen to achieve a good or excellent CPA result, they will typically look to the chief executive to propose ways of doing so.

> In the first inspection (2002), shortly after the Conservatives gained power, the council scored 4 for service and 2 for corporate governance. The new leader was keen for us to achieve an excellent rating, not least for the personal kudos this would involve. I drafted an action plan of 10 things that needed to be done, which were readily agreed by the leadership. I was 'pushing at an open door'.

In another case, the chief executive observed that

> The Labour leadership saw the value of getting a good CPA result, and there was nothing in their priorities which would have jeopardised the prospect of this outcome.

In other cases, however, chief executives reported a degree of political indifference to the CPA process, and how it affected their authority.

> *In both the authorities where I have been chief executive, the CPA rating was seen as irrelevant by leading members. Their priorities were not those of the government (nor the Audit Commission) and they saw no reason to modify them.*
>
> *The 2003 CPA verdict was 'fair', which I thought was generous! The politicians seemed quite happy with 'fair' and haven't sought a reassessment since.*

It may be significant that each of the authorities involved were small-medium district councils, who perhaps feel less threatened by the CPA process than higher-profile unitary or county councils. Even amongst small DCs, however, a poor classification, involving the label of 'a failing authority' is something to be avoided, not least because of the enhanced external scrutiny and influence it engenders, through the mechanisms of central government-imposed 'improvement plans' and 'recovery boards'.

One of the key influences on the CPA assessment is the visit by the team of inspectors, which involves, inter alia, a succession of meetings with leading members and officers. Several chief executives mentioned the importance of orchestrating the behaviour of council members and officers, so that the best possible impression is given, and the dangers of disruptive behaviour or conflicting messages are avoided. Varying degrees of success were reported.

> *There was a lot more preparation for the second (2004) CPA visit. After some pretty intensive coaching of members, we manage to achieve an 'excellent' although there was a hiccup when a 'critical appraisal' of the authority by the opposition leader was leaked.*
>
> *The main problem with the CPA process the second time around was when Labour tried to discredit the new regime and argued that the authority's performance had declined.*
>
> *The main challenge was to ensure that members were well-briefed, and that they behaved appropriately when the inspectors came...we were not entirely successful – party group leaders tended to blame their predecessors, and one leader totally mismanaged a key meeting in 2005.*

Whether or not to request a CPA reassessment – or to challenge an assessment if felt to be unfair – is an important strategic decision (or recommendation) which sometimes falls upon a chief executive.

> *We could have gone for a re-assessment in 2007, but we were warned we would be classified as poor... and we couldn't risk that in the light of the local reorganisation situation.*

> *I wanted to challenge a 'fair' CPA assessment which I considered was the result of an incompetent and biased inspection team. I had the full support of the leader in taking it up with the Audit Commission, who in the end admitted that they'd got it wrong, and moved us up a category.*

In the earlier research (see JRT (2005), Lowndes and Leach (2004) and Leach and Lowndes (2007)) several examples were found of chief executives seeking to persuade leaders to include in a strategy statement priorities other than those to which they were politically committed, to strengthen the chances of a positive CPA assessment. In the more recent interviews (2008–2009) there was little reference to this kind of chief executive intervention, perhaps because the scope for genuine strategic choice had narrowed (or was perceived to have narrowed) since the first half of the decade.

Expectations involved in the CPA

Strategic priorities

It was noted earlier that one of the Audit Commission's requirements in considering a positive CPA assessment is the existence of a clear set of priorities drawn together into a coherent corporate strategy. A review of the comments made about corporate strategies also suggests that the Audit Commission was looking (inter alia) for strategic priorities which reflected those of the government. It would be a risky corporate strategy which did not, for example, prioritise educational standards, partnership working, dealing with crime and disorder, and (in urban areas) economic regeneration, even in circumstances where there was a (perfectly legitimate) view from an administration that it did not share these priorities.

All the chief executives interviewed recognised the need for some form of coherent corporate strategy. Some (but not all) felt it important to reflect government priorities as well as (indeed, sometimes instead of) those of the dominant political party or parties.

Thus the first challenge, in the face of an impending CPA inspection, was to ensure that an appropriate corporate strategy was in place. In politicised authorities, the starting point would typically be the manifesto of the dominant party (or coalition partners), although this may be felt to need some interpretation (or fine-tuning) to transform it into a coherent strategy. But what if the party concerned does not have a document from which strategic priorities can be read off? Or there is a shared administration amongst three parties with different sets of priorities?

In the first case, the onus will be on a chief executive to produce a strategy which is compatible with priorities of the dominant party, even when these have not been made explicit. One chief executive interviewed was well aware of this challenge.

> *There was little in the way of strategic direction coming from the coalition.... But I knew enough about the priorities of the two parties concerned from the conversations with the leaders to be able to draft a strategy which proved politically acceptable.*

Another chief executive in a small shire district reported different experiences with different political groups.

> *Labour were clear about what they wanted to achieve...but the Conservatives had much less in the way of a clear vision...this meant that I had to be more proactive. I knew we had to have clear strategic priorities.... I had to tease out the values of the new administration, and what they would and wouldn't be likely to go along with.*

What is typically involved in developing political values into a set of strategic priorities likely to be acceptable to the CPA inspectors is a process of negotiation, assuming, of course, that leading politicians recognise the importance of strategic priorities and are prepared to negotiate. This is often a problematical process, as one of the JRF (2005) interviewees noted.

> *The new leader tended to avoid the big decisions, and strategy drifted for 3 years under his leadership...as the CPA visit*

approached, I made it clear that unless we had an explicit corporate strategy, we would get hammered by the inspection team. The Labour group then produced one which had too many priorities – everything seemed to be a priority. It just about got us through the inspection, but in my view it was never a viable document.

In another case

> There were difficulties in 2005–06 when very little strategic direction was coming from the Labour leadership... my response was to organise a one day seminar for all members to agree a set of priorities.

I raised the question of whether this process in effect 'defined out' political differences and therefore resulted in a managerial document. The chief executive's response was the level of generality of the priorities was such that you could get all-party agreement. Party differences emerged later in relation to *how* the priorities were achieved.

The advantages of having a strategy, – albeit at a high level of generality – which has the support of all parties was echoed by another chief executive.

> What has helped to hold things together in a difficult political climate has been the fact that all parties have signed up to our long-term strategy. It was drawn up in the 1990s through a series of all-party policy seminars... it meant that when the CPA process hit us there was already an agreed strategy and a performance management system in place.

Having a strategy which impresses the CPA inspectors is one thing; turning it into a reality is another! One chief executive agreed with the view that it is important for chief executives to find ways of influencing the strategic agendas but emphasised that there could be problems in ensuring that the strategy was both widely accepted and influential.

> There were two priorities when I arrived – improving education standards and improving highways, both of which were widely accepted. However there were many gaps... and also a fragmentation within the cabinet and the management team. Director/cabinet member pairings operated by and large as separate units.

This chief executive's response was to instigate an 'away weekend', away from the council offices, where a discussion amongst cabinet members could be facilitated in a relaxed atmosphere and the chief executive was able to feed in some ideas of her own. Other chief executives used similar types of occasions, sometimes to cajole reluctant party groups into thinking strategically, and often using the threat of an impending CPA visit as an incentive.

CPA inspectors – and hence chief executives – will usually wish to see evidence that a strategy – however impressive on paper – is actually influencing budget allocations. One chief executive had developed a mechanism for linking the strategy to the budget, which proved particularly influential in discussions with politicians at a crucial stage.

> *The Policy/Budget reconciliation process really began to blossom under the new administration. One of their electoral priorities was keeping council tax low. But I managed to persuade the leader that if they wanted to transform adult social services, they had to put money into it, and that would mean an increase in council tax. The leader agreed, with the provision that in the following three years, council tax increases would be very small.*

Another example of the kind of negotiations which take place regarding the link between strategic priorities and the budget was provided.

> *I had to warn the new administration that there was very little scope in the budget for priorities which would require a significant level of spending, in the wake of the financial crisis in the previous year ... the group accepted this and came up with six priorities – 'the Big 6' – all relatively modest – things like extra wardens on housing estates ...*

In summary, the expectations associated with the CPA process have resulted in an increasing concern on the part of chief executives that there should be in place a viable corporate strategy (with some – but not too many – priorities) and, since 2003 a community strategy (endorsed by the Local Strategic Partnership (LSP)) which is consistent with the corporate strategy. In both cases a 'reasonable' degree of congruence with central government priorities is usually seen as desirable. Prior to the introduction of CPA, corporate strategies, though still widely viewed by chief executives as 'good management practice', were less crucial to the reputation of an authority (and its ability to avoid detailed central government intervention) than they have since become. This new emphasis on corporate strategy has put pressure on chief executives to ensure first that there is such a document – which sometimes requires a teasing out and interpretation of political values and priorities – and second that the content is at least acceptable (in the light of experiences with or expectations of inspectors' views) – which sometimes involves negotiation with politicians over additions to (or deletions from) previously – identified political priorities. As we have seen, the kind of interpretations and negotiations involved are by no means straightforward, and in some cases chief executives have had little choice but to accept a distinctly sub-optimal outcome.

Performance management systems

A second expectation which emerges clearly from an analysis of CPA reports is that there should be in place a robust performance management system (PMS) whereby each service – whether provided by the council itself or in partnership with other agencies – can be monitored on a regular basis to check whether it is achieving agreed performance targets, and to initiate remedial action in the cases where it is failing to do so.

Chief executives recognised that they would be expected to take the lead on this matter. To a large extent the development of a PMS is a matter for negotiation between chief executives, directors and service heads. One chief executive explained in a failing authority how she tackled this challenge.

> *I emphasised at an early stage that it was part of my job to deal with poorly-performing managers.... I decided to run 'performance clinics' where heads of service were asked to explain poor performance and to show what they were doing to improve it...politicians were allowed to observe these clinics, but not to contribute...my view was that in the first stage I needed to protect officers from member scrutiny...once they'd got their act together then they could be exposed to members...*

However, there is a perceived need to achieve some degree of political commitment to a scheme of this nature, as illustrated by the following CPA comment (illustrated in the Audit Commission's CPA report on Worcestershire CC (2003)).[2]

> There is little evidence that members are challenging the performance information in a way which will enable the council to achieve its ends.

The problem is that performance monitoring and management are not topics which readily capture local politicians' imagination. There are increasing numbers of authorities which have introduced 'traffic light' or 'smiling/neutral/frowning faces' systems to enable politicians to more easily identify successes and problem areas. In some cases cabinets have begun to play the kind of challenging role expected of them; in others overview and scrutiny committees have done so. However, it remains a largely managerially-dominated process. The problem is that in dealing with performance issues, the tradition (and preference) in many authorities is for members to intervene – in one way or another – over particular cases, a phenomenon widely referred to as 'micromanagement', rather than review detailed tabulations of performance data. The implications of this problem for leader/chief executive relations are discussed in the next section.

'Members set policy: officers implement it'?

A third 'expectation' of CPA inspectors was that there should be a minimal involvement – if any – of councillors in day-to-day decision making.

> Under the previous administration, political leadership dominated, and was too heavily involved in day-to-day decision making.
>
> (North Tyneside 2003)

This expectation is a reflection of long-established dictum that members (should) decide policy and officers implement it. Day-to-day management, decision-making and policy implementation should be left to officers, operating within the policy guidelines set by members. The problems experienced in several authorities in meeting this expectation reflect the equally well-established tradition that members see it as a legitimate part of their role to involve themselves in policy implementation and detailed decision-making to varying extents, and in varying circumstances.

The tension between these sometimes very different sets of expectations (Audit Commission/chief executive vis-à-vis political leadership) can be a source of real problems for chief executives. The one example of a chief executive amongst the 16 interviewed who felt he could not continue in a particular authority was caused by member interference in micromanagement. A second chief executive had contemplated resigning in similar circumstances, and a third explained how in his previous authority, faced with the new leader there, who had a proclivity for micromanagement, he too would have resigned.

Whilst the majority of chief executives interviewed expressed a view that was in line with the traditional 'member make policy/officers implement it' dictum, some felt that this position was unrealistic.

> *It is entirely appropriate for councillors to wish to understand service delivery issues, particularly when they are the subject of complaints from people in their wards ... in this authority, chief officers and service heads are expected to consult with portfolio holders about delegated decisions which have a political dimension.*

It is likely that most chief executives would accept this view – certainly the first point, and probably the second point, so long as there existed a clear mechanism for dealing with disagreements which emerged from the consultation process. I asked the chief executive quoted above what would happen if a head of service, having consulted a portfolio holder disagreed with the decision which the latter wished him or her to make.

> *They would try to seek a compromise. If that did not prove possible, then the matter would go to the relevant director, or, alternatively, to me. I would then try to resolve it with the leader.*

A similar approach was adopted by another chief executive, albeit on a less frequent basis.

There have been occasions when I've had to say to leaders 'I think you are trespassing into my territory'... and occasions when leaders have said the same to me (or words to that effect). When this happens, I'll sit down with the leader and try to resolve the situation.

Consultation processes of the type described in the first example constitute a distinctly 'grey area'. In authorities where a range of executive decisions are delegated to area committees, the uncertainty is resolved by the fact that local councillors have been given the constitutional power to take decisions which (in authorities without area committees) would normally be seen as an officer responsibility. In such authorities, however, there may still be a residual problem of 'undue pressure'.

Because of our area committee system, there is less reason for members to put pressure on officers regarding detailed decisions... but it does still happen (over a decision not delegated to area committees) and I have to intervene from time to time.

It is not unusual for proactive leaders to wish to 'progress chase' over issues of particular importance to them, and to seek to set up mechanisms which enable them to do so.

The leader does have a desire to progress chase. We were both aware that there was a 'coasting culture' in many schools in the county and 'challenge to schools' had been part of the Conservative manifesto... with my approval, the leader set up a small group of members to review progress... it wasn't like an inquisition – indeed the Director of Children's Services welcomed it – more a case of selective performance monitoring; 'what progress have you made since the last meeting?'

A chief executive interviewed in the 2005 JRF project was somewhat more uneasy about a leader setting up a mechanism of this nature, but soon recognised its value. He drew attention to the determination of the new leader to pursue his personal manifesto promise to 'clean up the borough'. Because this was such a key priority for him, the leader decided to chair the officer task force charged with implementing the 'Operation Springclean' programme. This was a new precedent in the authority and there was initially a good deal of unease amongst chief officers (including the Chief Executive). However, the approach proved effective and initial doubts were quickly assuaged.

Chief executives who have been brought in to turn round a failing authority are more likely to be in a position to insist on a retreat from members' involvement on micromanagement.

> *There was a tradition in the authority of members interfering in detailed matters. I made it clear at an early meeting with the leader that I expected to be allowed to get on with delivering, once priorities had been decided, without interference of this nature.*

In another failing authority, the newly appointed chief executive soon realised that the 'micromanagement' tendencies of members were, in once sense, understandable.

> *The reason members involved themselves in detail was that they had very little involvement in the formulation of policy or strategy. The officers approach had been to keep them out of it until a relatively late stage, when it was difficult for them to do more than require marginal changes.... I saw my job as to bring members back into policy development, and steer them away from an involvement in managerial detail...*

This aim was achieved, although it did take time for members to withdraw from micromanagement.

Although there are authorities where member's involvement in micromanagement is not a problem, if there exists a strong tradition of this nature, it may be difficult, even with the invocation of Audit Commission expectations for a chief executive to change this culture in the short term.

Where the 'problem' persists, it is advantageous if there are clear guidelines – formally set out or informally agreed – which regulate the involvement of members in detail. The worst scenario is one where there is an arbitrary and unregulated pattern of member involvement of this nature, and/or an informal rule of officers consulting portfolio holders over operational decisions, without clear mechanisms for dealing with the differences of view which will inevitably emerge from time to time. The need to find some way of dealing with this division of labour is particularly pressing in mayoral authorities, where mayors will understandably wish to develop the capacity to deliver for local people on detailed issues.

Partnership working

There are similarities – and differences – between the Audit Commissions concerns about performance management and partnership working. The former is a largely internal operation, and although the involvement and commitment of politicians is a bonus, the function can operate effectively as a management-dominated activity. Partnership working, however, does require the active (and positive) involvement of leading members if it is to be effective (not least because other partners' attitudes will be adversely affected by the indifference/antagonism of local council leaders).

> Frequently partners' experience is that the council uses partnerships reluctantly, and only when it cannot deliver sources or activities in house.
>
> (Kingston upon Hull (2003))

However, the lack of political enthusiasm noted in relation to performance management was in the early mid-2000s also apparent in relation to partnership working, with the added edge of a resentment that other 'partners' had 'taken over' functions previously the responsibility of council

> Both main parties have struggled with the partnership concept – the current opposition leader doesn't attend the LSP, even though he knows I think it would be beneficial if he did. I have really had to work to make successive council leaders understand how important partnership working has become.
>
> There's a problem with partnership working here. The leading politicians don't like partnerships...the leader chairs the LSP, but has no real commitment to it.... I chair the Crime and Disorder Partnership only because the members have no interest in doing so.

Other comments echoed these sentiments

> Members couldn't see the point of it (partnership working). Their priority was to put the council's own house in order. I ended up chairing

the key partnership – including the LSP – myself. It wasn't ideal and we had criticism in our second CPA about the lack of leadership from councillors.

Other chief executives had more success in convincing leading members of the importance of partnership working. One chief executive managed to convince a sceptical new leader of the importance of the partnership arrangements in the metropolitan area concerned, so much so that the leader became an enthusiastic advocate for them. Another noted that she had had to push the importance of partnership working with a Labour group not predisposed to it. Ultimately her persuasion was effective and 'everyone now sees the importance'.

Once the barriers of political indifferences or hostility have been overcome, there is an issue to be faced of what the role in partnership working should be of leader and chief executive respectively.

There is a clear division of labour between the leader and I ... wherever there is a public platform, it is the leader who takes the lead. So he chairs the strategic partnership, the Crime and Disorder Partnership etc ... my focus is internal; ensuring that the organisational culture delivers what the politicians want.

After a period of uncertainty, there is now a working arrangement whereby the leader chairs the LSP executive, and I chair the delivery agency of the partnership.

There is of course scope for leading members other than the council leader to chair service-specific partnerships (e.g. a Children's Trust), although there may in some cases be an argument for an officer (or an 'independent' partner representative) to chair bodies such as these (as the examples discussed in Chapter 8 illustrate).

Generally the basis for the political/managerial division of labour is seen to be the extent to which the partnership deals with service delivery as opposed to strategic planning issues. If the latter (as in LSPs), it is felt appropriate for the leader to chair; if the former, then the chief executive, or the appropriate service director.

Public and customer involvement

There are two key elements to CPA expectations regarding public/customer involvement. The first is that authorities should demonstrate a readiness to consult the public and incorporate public priorities into council strategies; the second is that a 'responsiveness to customers' should also be demonstrated. In relation to the first of these elements:

> the choice of (the council's) priorities is not based on comprehensive public consultation.
>
> (Worcs CC 2003)
>
> the corporate plan is not clearly focused on local peoples' priorities.
>
> (North Shropshire DC 2004)

'Responsiveness to customers' is a long-standing expectation which predates the Labour election win in 1997 and was articulated in the 'Best Value' project. Its importance to chief executives was illustrated by a question asked by one chief executive shortly after I arrived for the interview, 'What was your experience at the customer reception desk?' The reasons for her concern later became apparent.

> *When I was appointed, I soon realised that there was little concern in the authority about how our customers were treated. I realised that a major change of culture was required...*

Other chief executives identified similar priorities

> *We were not good at consulting the public. I devised some imaginative ways of consulting the public over priorities, and that is now built in to the way we do things here.*

> *We have now developed an all-party consensus about the importance of public involvement... although different parties have different interpretations about what this involves.*

Conclusion

'Enhancing public involvement' provides a further example of how chief executives can use expectations built into the CPA process to argue for changes in structures, processes and culture – in some cases because they personally believe in them as good management practice (e.g. the examples on public involvement set out above all reflected chief executives' own values); in others because they saw them as essential ingredients to a 'good' result (e.g. a coherent corporate strategy, a robust PMS). Such attempts to persuade members of the value of changes in structures, processes or culture are, of course, not new. What *is* new is the ability to use the reference point of impending CPA inspections to strengthen the arguments. It is no longer just a case of 'I as your chief executive think we ought to have a corporate strategy'. It is 'the Audit Commission will expect us to have a corporate strategy... and we run the risk of getting a weak or poor result if we don't have one... and you know what that would mean!' In this situation, the negotiating position of chief executives has been considerably strengthened, although it can still be countered by the arguments such as 'we don't care about the CPA', 'we've no intention of taking public consultation seriously' or 'we are a "hands-on" group and we don't intend to change!'

11
The Impact of the Move to Executive Government

Introduction

The 2000 Local Government Act introduced an executive system of local government which parallels that of central government. Policy and the budget have to be agreed by full council (just as legislation has to be passed by Parliament). The executive (whether led by a mayor or council leader) then has the authority to take executive decisions within this policy/budgetary framework.

There are two potential major impacts of this move to local executive government for councillor/officer relationships. First, the 2000 Act, on the face of it, provides the opportunity for councillors who are members of the executive to increase the scope of their decision responsibilities beyond the norm which prevailed under the old committee system (which was premised on the 'members set policy/officers implement it' distinction, although with many variations of interpretation). Secondly, it has placed considerable strain on the principle of the 'unified officer structure' in which officers, at all levels, are required to serve 'the whole council' as well as 'the administration'.

One or two chief executives amongst those interviewed felt strongly that it was now more difficult for a chief executive to serve the whole council than it was prior to the 2000 Local Government Act.

> *I do my best to play this role – for example through the opposition briefing meetings – but in reality I spend most of my time serving the leadership group. I've become more like a civil servant.*

This chief executive went on to speculate that in time, chief executives and other directors will be political appointments, as in the United States, resigning if the party in power changes.

Although there were echoes of this view in the interviews with other chief executives, it was significant how few of them referred to the challenge of serving the whole council, under the executive system, as a problem. As noted in Chapter 4, several chief executives emphasised the importance of keeping opposition groups informed, using mechanisms such as joint leaders meetings, opposition leader briefings or the readiness (on request) to attend meetings of opposition group as well as the dominant party. But that was as far as it went. It was as though little had actually changed, following the introduction of cabinet government. If more authorities had taken the opportunity to 'claw back' areas of decision-making previously delegated to officers and allocate then to portfolio-holders (including leaders), then more problems would be likely to have been perceived by chief executives. But (with very few exceptions) this has not happened. In practice, the transition from the pre-2000 Act system – with the Policy and Resource Committee the focus of decision-making – to local executive government has been more cosmetic than seismic. True Policy and Resources Committees had to be 'balanced' with proportional representation from other parties. But in reality, the real business was done in preparatory meetings between chief officers and majority group members of the Policy and Resources Committee (typically comprising most or all of the committee chairs). This practice has continued under the executive system, with the equivalent to the Policy and Resources Committee being the public meeting of the Cabinet (required by law) at which the decisions reached at the private cabinet meeting the previous week are in effect ratified, sometimes with the facility for opposition members to ask questions. In effect, little has changed beyond a superficial reshuffling of titles and forums.

What has changed, in many although by no means all authorities, is the extent to which the relationship between chief executive and leader has increased in importance. This change has been partly influenced by the government's growing belief in the value of 'strong' leadership, and the way they have sought to embed this value in legislative terms – particularly the provisions of the 2007 Act which formally allocate various powers to leaders (selection of cabinet colleagues and portfolio allocation) and on the face of it, provides them with a 4-year 'security of tenure'. However, leaders were becoming increasingly dominant in all parties, well before the 2000 Act and the government's current obsessions (see Widdicombe (1986), Leach and Wilson (2000)) and it is likely that this trend would have continued without these further incentives.

Increasingly, chief executives are being faced with leaders who are trusted or expected by their groups to lead in a pro-active fashion (or have established a precedent for doing so). That situation is of benefit to chief executives, so long as they can establish a trusting relationship, where both are 'open to influence' and both recognise that their future success (in the different spheres in which they operate) is interconnected. In my judgement, 10 of the 16 chief executives interviewed enjoyed a relationship of this nature, where additionally the chief executive could rely on the leader to deliver the group (or to recognise when he or she could not,) and the leader could rely on the chief executive to deliver his or her priorities (or to explain when and why this was not possible).

In the other cases, there were reasons why the leader could not or would not operate in this way. In one case the requisite element of mutual trust and the ability to sort out problems was not present. In the others, the leader typically lacked the requisite skills (e.g. found it difficult to persuade group colleagues to accept a course of action agreed with the chief executive) or did not see the need to do so, when the need (from the chief executive's perspective) clearly existed.

> *Because the leader doesn't provide much in the way of strategic leadership, the cabinet does not always behave as a collective entity...members sometimes feel free to do their own thing...they'll agree a policy at one meeting and then oppose it publicly at another.*
>
> *Problems have emerged with the increasing dominance of the Conservative group. The leader finds it more difficult to get her own way. Her position as group leader has been weakened, and I can't get access to the group in the way I used to be able to...*

In two cases, reading between the lines of the interviews, there was a strong impression of an assertive chief executive with a clear agenda of her own being in a dominant position in relation to a less assertive leader with a more diffuse agenda.

The challenge of overview and scrutiny

One of the areas where the continued viability of the unified officer structure (and the chief executive's role within it) appeared particularly vulnerable after the Local Government Act 2000 was the overview and scrutiny function. A CfPA report on the political dimensions of overview and scrutiny makes this clear.

> The crucial political relationship for a director is of course with the one or more portfolio holders whose responsibilities match those of the director. All directors have a 'professional' view of what should be done in their field of expertise. They will seek to convince these portfolio holder(s) whom they brief of the appropriateness of policies and decisions within their remit, within the context of the political priorities adopted by the majority group or coalition concerned. It is a process of negotiation. Once the negotiation has been resolved, portfolio holder and director have a common interest in maximising the probability of the acceptance of the outcome at cabinet/directors board level. In this context, the possibility of challenge from an overview and scrutiny panel is likely to seem as an obstacle, rather than potential benefit.
>
> (Leach 2009, p. 7)

This tension applies equally to the range of policies/decisions which fall within the ambit of the chief executive and leader. The main reference point for the chief executive (and other directors) under the executive system is inevitably going to be the cabinet, rather than the overview and scrutiny function. Indeed there will be a temptation, in certain circumstances for the latter to be viewed by leading members and officers alike as something of a nuisance, challenging carefully – researched cabinet decisions, or arguing for non-viable alternatives or inappropriate policies.

This tension was well-illustrated by an early review of overview and scrutiny which I carried out in 2002–2003 in an authority which shall remain nameless. The main opposition leader, during my interview with him, had expressed real concern at the marginalisation of the opposition (as he saw it) within the overview and scrutiny arrangements, and claimed that if changes were not made, he would 'shop the council' in the forthcoming CPA inspection. It was not clear what the basis would be of this potentially disruptive intervention. But in any event, I felt it was appropriate to recommend a re-allocation of chairs of overview and scrutiny committees to include some opposition members (at the time, the majority party held all such chairs). The chief executive, after consulting the leader, was unhappy with this recommendation and asked me to delete it.

In the end an unsatisfactory compromise form of wording was agreed, to ensure (from my perspective) that the report was not sidelined, and that the opportunity for an all-party debate on the other recommendations was preserved. Whether the opposition leader carried out his threat I do not know. But I suspect if his group had gained power at the next election, he might well have had serious reservations about whether he could operate with the chief executive who had been so uncooperative to the group when in opposition.

Although the problem-generating potential of overview and scrutiny for chief executive/leader relationships is apparent, illustrated by the previous example (what would have happened if the chief executive had been convinced by my eminently reasonable arguments and made it a 'bottom-line' issue with the leader?), there was relatively little reference by the chief executives interviewed to overview and scrutiny as a 'problem area'. When I raised the issue, the explanation typically given (not always convincingly) was that overview and scrutiny was operating in the authority in a way which was acceptable to opposition members. In some cases opposition members chaired some (or all) of the scrutiny committees. In others they had been steered into policy development/review work on topics which the cabinet was 'prepared to be influenced'. In some (relatively) sizeable scrutiny support units had been established. In one or two there was a genuine openness to challenge and influence on the part of the leadership of the dominant group. There are various mechanisms through which the disruptive potential of overview and scrutiny for the dominant group can be minimised (see Leach (2009, pp. 10–12)). Thus, in general, the challenge to the viability of the unified officer structure (and the role of chief executive in 'serving the whole council') has remained latent.

Chief executives have to take overview and scrutiny seriously because comments are invariably made in CPA reports about the effectiveness of such arrangements. For example

> The scrutiny process is not effective across all committees and has rarely resulted in serious challenge to executive members.
> (Blackburn and Darwen 2003)

> Overview and scrutiny arrangements provide meaningful roles for non-cabinet members. Policy development responsibilities of overview and scrutiny are strongly supported by backbench members and provide valuable support to portfolio holders.
> (LB Westminster 2003)

The scope for interpretation implied by these mixed messages (is the primary role of overview and scrutiny to challenge the executive or support it?) is apparent, as chief executives quickly realised after the first set of CPA inspection reports were issued. It also soon became apparent that a critical assessment of the overview and scrutiny function did not have an impact on the overall classification. Several 'excellent' councils (particularly counties) received this rating despite a highly critical analysis of their overview and scrutiny function.

'The dog that isn't barking'

Whereas the introduction of the CPA regime was likely to have increased the potential influence of chief executives (vis-a-vis political leaders) the reverse was true in relation to local executive government. In particular two major threats to the traditional basis for the relationship were identified; the opportunity for cabinet members to develop a more hands-on role, through the allocation of decision powers to individuals, and the potential difficulties for a chief executive in supporting 'executive' and 'overview and scrutiny' roles equally (or in a way which approaches equality!)

It is helpful to consider in a bit more detail why such problems have not developed – why 'the dog hasn't barked'. The way in which the potential threat of overview and scrutiny has been neutralised or marginalised was discussed in the previous section (in addition there remains a good deal of confusion amongst all members about what role or roles overview and scrutiny is supposed to be playing). But why has the switch to a hands-on micromanagement role not taken place, apart from some mayoral authorities and a few others?

The Local Government Act 2000 provided flexibility for a wide range of ways of dealing with executive decisions. At one extreme, it would only be major executive decisions which would be the responsibility of cabinet members. The concept of 'key decisions' (financial threshold typically around £500K; and/or impact on more than one ward) often provides the basis for identifying cabinet responsibilities, although it is legal (and a matter of practice in some authorities) for some key decisions, as defined in the constitution, to be delegated to officers. At the other extreme, it would be possible for a whole range of executive decisions which would previously have been delegated to officers now to be identified on decisions to be taken by the cabinet. In these circumstances it would be apparent that the balance of power had moved, in relative terms, from officers to councillors. As the Audit Commission (2001) warned:

> One of the consequences of the enhanced visibility of members that the directly elected mayor model, and to a slightly lesser degree, the leader model brings is to place leading members in a much more visible, direct-contact relationship with the community. Feeling the strength of the public contract, leading members are more likely to feel the need to ensure that the council delivers. Indeed, it is quite likely that a mayor will have campaigned on a programme of action therefore, almost inevitably, becoming involved in executive activity.

Do elected mayors make a difference?

The above quote from the Audit Commission suggests that there might be significant differences between the chief executive/elected mayor relationship, on the one hand, and the chief executive/council leader relationship, on the other, because of two related factors. The direct election of mayors as individuals means that (in theory) they can be held personally accountable by the electorate for a wide range of executive decisions. As a result, there is a likelihood that mayors will wish to take formal responsibility for a wider range of such decisions than a council leader might wish to adopt, thus changing the traditional distribution of responsibilities between council leader (strategic decisions) and chief executive (operational decisions). The differences between the two executive forms have reduced as a result of the 2007 Local Government Act, which gave leaders for the first time the power to decide the range of executive decisions for which they wished to have responsibility. However, there is less of an incentive for them to do so, because unlike mayors, they will not be standing for re-election as individuals.

The reality is that much depends on the attitude and previous experience of the elected mayors. If they have no previous experience of council leadership, they are likely to judge that it would be premature to take on a wide range of executive responsibility, at least during the first couple of years when they are settling in to the job. If at the time of their election they were already in position as council leader, then they will have been working to an established divisions of responsibilities with the chief executive, and may lack the incentive to change this arrangement even though in theory they could. There will of course be exceptions to this general tendency. A newly elected mayor who has little or no experience of council leadership may nonetheless feel confident enough to seek a wide executive remit. There may also be experienced 'in post' leaders who seek and achieve mayoral status with a view to 'breaking the mould', in a way which involves a new (mayor-oriented) balance of responsibilities between mayor and chief executive. In both these situations, however, the newly elected mayor in 2001/2 may well have been constrained in his or her ability to make these kind of changes by the content of the constitution, which is likely to have been agreed before the mayoral election. As one chief executive in a mayoral authority told us in the 2005 JRF research.

> The constitution was drawn up in this authority in a way which protected the council's interests. The mayor is permitted virtually no virement powers.

It should also be borne in mind that, in England, the responsibility for appointing the chief executive has remained with the council, and has not been transferred to the elected mayor, following the local Government Act 2000. In authorities where the party to which the mayor is affiliated is also dominant on the council, and the mayor is a dominant figure within his or her group, then it is likely that the mayor will be able to ensure (or strongly influence) the appointment of his or her preferred candidate. However, in other cases, where there is not a political congruence of this nature, it will not be possible for the mayor to exert the same degree of influence; indeed if there is a tense or conflictual relationship between mayor and council, then his or her degree of influence may be negligible. Similar differences would exist in relation to seeking to change a sitting chief executive. Elected mayors could not seek to do so in their mayoral capacity; they would need the support of the council, which would be much more likely to be forthcoming in a situation of political congruence between mayor and council, than if there was a mismatch of party affiliations. That is not to say that a chief executive who found it increasingly difficult to work with an elected mayor antagonistic to his or her continued presence might not soon seek a more comfortable post elsewhere. But they could not be forced to do so.

Six chief executives of mayoral authorities were interviewed as part of the JRF research (2005). Of these, four were working with relatively inexperienced mayors, who inevitably relied heavily upon them, in the same way that a newly elected and inexperienced council leader would do. Of the two other mayors involved, one did have previous experience of council leadership (although not in the period leading up to the mayoral election) and the other was a charismatic individual who, even though he had had no previous experience of council leadership (nor, indeed, council membership), did have a clear vision of the area and a strong sense of his capacity to ensure that it was delivered.

In his authoritative research-based study of elected mayors in England, Copus (2006) makes a helpful distinction between three broad types of elected mayor; the visionary, the insider and the gradualist.

> The *visionary* is the mayor who is determined to make a difference to the conduct of politics on the council and to the broader local political environment: he or she has a clearly articulated view of how politics should change and envisions a more inclusive and participatory set of political process. Furthermore, the visionary is not afraid to see the political party dislodged from its dominant position locally. The visionary may prompt argument and disagreement and may even court controversy, but it is done with

a clear view that such action stimulates and helps maintain public engagement and interest in the political process. What marks out the visionary is the action he or she takes to stimulate an all-encompassing political climate locally. What drives the mayor is the desire to create a new style of local politics and a belief that the office of directly elected mayor is the most powerful tool by which to achieve this aim.

(Copus 2006, p. 194–5)

Copus notes that three of the 11 elected mayors in England (excluding the GLA) could be seen as visionaries. The last two examples of my elected mayor interviewees (see above) would certainly fit into this category. The 'insider' mayor provides something of a contrast.

The *insider*, as the name implies, is at home with the conduct of politics, both on and off the council, as they were before the advent of the office of elected mayor. Such a mayor sees no great advantage or disadvantage from the creation of a different style of politics and understands, and is able to work within, a political system dominated by political parties and a largely disengaged citizenry. The insider sees the office of mayor as ideally suited to enabling him or her to negotiate the deals and support required to pursue political initiatives and policy preferences, as well as to dealing with the day-to-day running of the council.

The insider sets out not to radically change the conduct of local politics but rather to ensure that the existing processes are developed to accommodate the new office and to recognise the role and position that go with that office. Moreover, the insider is concerned to ensure that the office of mayor accrues as much political power as possible to play the existing political game, while respecting the existing status quo of organisation and structure and wishing, as far as possible, to avoid political controversy.

(Copus 2006, p. 195)

The sense of continuity involved with 'insider' mayors is illustrated by a telling interview quote in Copus's book (ibid, p. 196)

The mayor was leader before he became mayor and all that's changed is what we call him.

There is also a sense of continuity and incremental rather than radical change implied in the way Copus characterises the gradualist mayor.

> The *gradualist* welcomes the opportunity for a new style of politics that the office of elected mayor potentially provides, but does not see the sole purpose of the mayoral office as that of ushering in a new dawn of local political activity. Rather, the gradualist opts for business as usual, unless specific areas of the political decision-making processes within the council require change and development. Moreover, the gradualist views the interaction between council and citizenry from a very pragmatic point of view – what works stays, and what does not work stays until it becomes necessary to change it.
>
> The gradualist sees politics – much like the insider – as the politics of the council and the council acting with the citizenry. The gradualist has no long-term agenda to change politics in any way other than incrementally.
>
> (Copus 2006, p. 196)

None of my interviewees fell into the insider category, primarily because none of them had held positions of power within the authority in the period preceding the mayoral election. Three were total outsiders, whilst two had had limited experience of council activity as members of a minority party.[1]

If the four who were not 'visionaries' fitted into any of Copus's three categories it would be the 'gradualist' mainly because they lacked the experience (and initially the confidence) to pursue any path other than gradualism. There may indeed be an important further distinction to be made within this category, between the less experienced gradualist and the more experienced exponent of gradualism.

It is apparent that neither the insider not the gradualist is likely to wish to initiate radical changes to the traditional balance of responsibilities between leader and chief executive. One of the mayors interviewed by Copus did however make a strong case for more radical change.

> I am seriously considering the future of the chief executive post. I am not convinced we need a chief executive with an elected mayor. We must have someone to be head of paid service, but I as mayor, run this organisation.
>
> (quoted in Copus 2006, p. 91)

This however was an untypical view, just as the choice to reclassify chief executives as managing directors in one or two mayoral authorities has proved cosmetic rather than substantive.

For four inexperienced elected mayors whom I interviewed in 2004–2005, their relationship with the chief executive was crucial in enabling them to make an impact, particularly in three authorities where the council was suspicious of or downright antagonistic to the mayor concerned. In one example my interview notes contain the following observation.

> The reason for the chief executive's survival (in fraught personal circumstances) is that the mayor actually needs him. The mayor came into office with unrealistic expectations about the scope of his powers. He did not have the diplomatic skills to get his budget, or key policies, through a hostile council himself. The chief executive negotiated a compromise with the parties in the council, advised the mayor as to the deal he'd brokered, and the amended budget got through.

In another JRF (2005) example, the chief executive expressed a similar viewpoint.

> There is a high degree of trust in the relationship based on mutual dependency. The mayor's success is mine, and mine is hers.

In both examples the chief executive was involved in helping the elected mayor get policies and budget through a hostile council. Susan Law, the short-lived managing director of the mayor-led Doncaster MBC, expressed the view that she 'didn't have to manage the politics here' (*MJ* 14 October 2004). That was certainly not the view of the chief executives I interviewed in authorities where there was a mismatch between the mayor's political affiliation (or lack of them) and those of the majority of the council.

It can be concluded that the relationship between chief executives and elected mayors is (with only one or two exceptions) not as different as might be expected to that between chief executives and council leaders. It is not that structures and constitutional provisions are not influential; they clearly are. However, in the case of elected mayors – as in many other local authority examples – it is the way that the opportunities to use these powers are interpreted and exploited which is a stronger influence. It is not unusual for the weight of tradition to considerably limit the impact of structural or constitutional change.

Conclusion

The reality is that, although the potential for a major shift in the roles and responsibilities of leaders and chief executives respectively, as a result of the introduction of executive structure, clearly exists, it is quite rare for such a change to have taken place in practice even in authorities headed by elected mayors. This outcome is largely the result of a tendency on the part of executives to exercise their decision responsibilities on a collective basis, rather than allocating a significant proportion of them to individual portfolio holders (Gains et al. 2009). Clearly the scope for extending the range of councillor decision-making is greater, if there are significant individual decision-making powers for executive members. If this is not the case then the capacity of cabinet meetings to exercise executive authority over a wider range of decisions than these characterised as 'key decisions' would be very limited. It is true that 38 per cent of leaders following the 2000 Act had power to take decisions on an individual basis and this proportion might be expected to increase following the strengthening of council leaders' powers embodied in the 2007 Local Government Act. However except for the council leader, relatively little decision-making power has been allocated to cabinet members, probably initially because of the fear of surcharge with which such responsibilities would be associated. Even where delegation of this nature has taken place, it is often on a very limited scale. Overall there has been an increase since 2001 in the decision-making powers delegated to officers (Gains et al. 2009).

As noted earlier, the potential for this change in the balance of power towards leaders and cabinets remains, and has arguably been extended by the strengthening of the powers of individual leadership, as set out in the 2007 Act. In principle it would be possible for a leader to rescind officer delegation schemes for a whole raft of detailed decisions, and to re-allocate them to himself or herself and/or their selected cabinet colleagues. Whether or not this scenario is likely to develop is discussed in the next (and final) chapter.

12
Where Next for Chief Executives

An increasingly vulnerable job?

The overwhelming impression emanating from the interview material in Chapters 2–8 and 10–11 is one of chief executives who are managing reasonably effectively in a political environment. There were exceptions. One of the interviewees had recently resigned in response to an unmanageable relation with the leader; another did so shortly afterwards not for this reason, but rather because he felt he was becoming increasingly sidelined as a result of the changing dynamics of the majority group. But the remaining interviewees (and most of those interviewed in connection with 2003–2005 JRF research) had developed a relationship with the political leadership which enabled them to carry out the functions which they felt they needed to carry out, with a clear political steer (or in some cases acquiescence) and with an acceptable division of labour. In some cases they could not speak too highly of their relationship with the leader; however, it was more typical for there to be periodic disagreements and difficulties in the relationships, the underlying strength of which enabled satisfactory resolutions to be achieved.

A quite different impression is provided by the material in Chapter 9, which draws on reports in the local government press to paint a picture of leaders and chief executives falling out with each other, proving unable to find ways of resolving conflicts and (in many cases) deciding that a termination of the relationship is the only feasible solution.

The sample of cases discussed in Chapter 9 was not of course a random one. Examples of dysfunctional relationships were sought out as a means of increasing understanding of leader/chief executive relationships, through focusing upon the reasons why things go wrong, and the difficulties (in certain circumstances) of rectifying them when they do. The interviewees in the larger sample of 30 whose experiences were discussed in the earlier chapters, although not randomly selected, were not identified either because their relationships were reputedly co-operative or problematical. As noted earlier, of the current relationships of the interviewees about one-fifth was clearly proving difficult to manage (from the chief executive's perspective); about two-fifths experienced periodic tensions or misunderstandings which had (so far) been overcome, whilst the remainder had developed in a way which was viewed in positive terms by both chief executive and leader.[1] That kind of distribution is broadly in line with earlier studies (Leach, Pratchett and Wingfield (1997); Leach and Wilson (2000)). Most chief executives, most of the time, find a way of managing in a political environment which is at worst satisfactory and at best extremely rewarding.

There is however the issue of whether there are recent changes in the context within which leaders and chief executives currently operate which in some way put more pressure on the relationship, and hence make it more vulnerable and unstable. That is certainly the view of the influential 2006 SOLACE Report 'Managing in a Political Environment'.

> Evidence presented to the Committee indicated that there had been a significant rise in the past few years in the number of chief executives who were finding themselves in difficulties either with their leader, or with their councils more generally. A number of these cases have been high profile.... The Commission was concerned to try to identify why this was happening and how we could avoid the trend continuing.
> (SOLACE 2006, p. 34)

The 5/6 years preceding the Commission's report were indeed the period in which many of the particularly contentious cases discussed in Chapter 9 occurred (e.g. those in Kingston-upon-Hull, Lincolnshire, Liverpool, Cheltenham, North East Derbyshire,

Islington and Erewash). The SOLACE report rightly points out that 'often, though not always...the chief executives concerned have been totally or almost totally exonerated and received significant compensation payments'[2] (ibid, p. 34). In which case the question is raised as to why local politicians are falling out more readily with chief executives, when it appears there is little in their behaviour which justifies it.

Causes of breakdown in relationships

The Commission provides its own explanation. They identify a series of eight factors which they believe may have contributed to the trend (of increasing numbers of chief executives experiencing difficulties with their leaders or councils), which include the following possibilities (SOLACE 2006, p. 34–5).

- Increasingly officers are implementing programmes at the behest of government of which members do not approve, but in which they have little say. 'The officer-messenger is often the one shot at by the politicians...'.
- A poor CPA report may lead to speculation and unhelpful division between members and officers as to who was responsible and who should 'carry the can'.
- The lack of willingness of the political parties to manage behaviour.
- The ability of chief executives to complain about councillors to the Standards Board (linked to the existence of whistleblowing protection).
- The more active leading councillors produced by executive or mayor arrangements...where there is a leader or executive who prefers its own council to those of its officers, it entrenches their position, and make it more difficult for the chief executive and other senior officers to advise them properly...

Of these suggested causes, it can be argued that the first (implementing unpopular programmes) and the third (unwillingness to manage political behaviour) are not new and are on the face of it unlikely to have been affected by any of the legislation between 2000 and 2010.

The three remaining possible influences postulated by the Commission each reflects one particular aspect of the government's legislative programmes for local government. The CPA inspection system has already been identified as a potentially destabilising factor in chief executive/leader relationships (see Chapter 10). The establishment of the Standards Board and the whistleblowing responsibilities of council officers were key elements in the new ethical framework introduced under the Local Government Act 2000, and clearly featured in several of the examples of breakdown in chief executive/leader relationships discussed in Chapter 9. The final influence identified by the Commission refers to the impact of the introduction of new executives (discussed in Chapter 11) although it does so in a way which lacks clarity and (in so far as it can be deciphered) lacks conviction. Where is the evidence that leaders and executives are seeking, in effect, to bypass traditional sources of advice? To whom would any leader or executive who 'prefers its own counsel to that of officers' turn, to access the advice required to ensure that a decision is legal, financially sound and capable of implementation? Special advisors are very thin on the ground in local government (the GLA mayoral office excepted). In any local authority there is a mutual dependency in operation between the political and managerial leadership which even political regimes who were 'minded to go their own way' would inevitably have to recognise. It is more likely that the level of dependency of executive members on chief officers has actually increased, particularly in the 2000–2005 period, given the unfamiliarity of the 'portfolio holder' position and the exposure inexperienced cabinet members must have felt, in the face of such responsibilities. The move to local executive government did have an influence on chief executive/leader relationships, as discussed in Chapter 11, but rarely in the destabilising way suggested in the SOLACE report.

There is a major omission in the SOLACE list of influences which can destabilise chief executive/leader relationships and that is political change. We saw in Chapter 5 how a change of administration can create real problems for a chief executive. In particular, if he or she is viewed, rightly or wrongly, by the incoming administration as too closely – identified with its predecessors – then the chief executive faces a real challenge in convincing the new leadership that he or she can serve them equally well.

Such problems of persuasion are particularly significant when there are sharp ideological differences between the parties. The 1980s was a decade in which the polarisation between the Labour and Conservative parties was much sharper than it is now. The chief executive of LB Ealing, accustomed to a long period of Conservative control, told the leader of the new-elected Labour administration in 1986 that 'he didn't think he could deliver their manifesto'. Not surprisingly, he did not remain long in office, and the Labour leader operated as de facto chief executive for the next 2–3 years (Leach and Wilson 2000, p. 112). There were several similar examples, although it was rare for a chief executive to concede defeat in such a helpless fashion.

The 1990s and the first decade of the twenty-first century have not proved such an ideological battleground; indeed the 'competition for the middle ground' is the essence of the approaches of all three major parties. The battles between the (so-called) loony left and the increasingly 'dry' Conservatives, which were a feature of local London and provincial metropolitan area politics in the 1980s, have not survived the re-launch of the 'new Labour' in the mid-1990s. Thus political/ideological differences – one of the key destabilising influences on leader/chief executive relationships – are now much more muted. However, there remain examples of incoming Conservative administrations which mistrust chief executives who have implemented their opponents' priorities (see Chapter 5 for typical examples).

It is possible to identify, in a provisional way, which of these potential influences on the breakdown of leader/chief executive relationships have been most prevalent over the 2000–2006 period. Features of 26 cases of breakdown (or near breakdown) were identified from the pages of *MJ* and *LGC* over this period. In each case it was possible to identify the main cause of the problem, in four cases, two major causes could be identified. Table 12.1 shows the breakdown of causes involved.

This evidence tends to confirm the view expressed earlier that of the three new potential influences – CPA inspections, new whistleblowing responsibilities and the introduction of executive government – the first two have proved far more influential than the third. And in none of the cases which came under the category of 'introduction of executive government' is there an implication of 'leaders or executives who prefer their own counsel to those of its officers' (see Chapter 12, p. 166 above). Rather the political view is *either*

Table 12.1 Causes of breakdown in leader/chief executive relationships

Cause of breakdown	No of Authorities	Examples
Problems associated with critical CPA report	9	LB Hillingdon, NE Lincs, Tunbridge Wells, Hull City Council
Problems associated with whistleblowing misconduct, disciplinary issues etc	14	Lincs CC, Cheltenham DC, Waverley DC, Erewash DC
Problems associated with introduction of executive government	3	Thurrock UA, Bristol City Council
Problems associated with political change	4	LB Islington, Hull City Council

that a chief executive per se is no longer needed in the new political circumstances *or* that a managing director is a more appropriate form of lead officer support. The (occasional) practice of dispensing with a chief executive predates the introduction of cabinet government (North Tyneside introduced a collegiate form of directorate structure with no chief executive in the early 1990s) and is almost always reversed after a few years (North Tyneside in 2000: Bristol in 2003). The move to a managing director model (which is discussed further below) has sometimes been used as a basis for making an existing chief executive redundant, and not untypically involves only the sketchiest of understandings as to how the managing director role actually differs from that of a chief executive.

> Thurrock BC has become the latest authority to change the title of chief executive to that of managing director because of its new political structure...a council spokeswoman said 'the system now adopted by Thurrock gives true executive powers to the leader of the council and cabinet members. So this newly created position highlights the shifts in power and responsibility from officers towards elected members of the council...'.
>
> (*MJ* 25 January 2002)

One wonders if in due course anyone noticed the difference in the way the lead officer role was being carried out, irrespective of the change of title. Table 12.1 also shows that whereas political change is still a relevant influence on relationship breakdown, it has been overtaken in significance (compared with the 1980s) by CPA inspection and whistleblowing issues. Nonetheless the change of administration in Hull in 2003 was also a factor behind the easing out of Jim Brooks (see Chapter 9).

Of these various destabilising influences, the problems for chief executives resulting from government inspection processes are likely to reduce in significance now that the CPA has been replaced by the CAA (Comprehensive Area Assessment), the scope of which means that it would be much more difficult (and even less justifiable) to attribute blame to a chief executive if a critical report were to be issued. By implication a whole range of public agencies, including PCTs and the Police, would be collectively responsible. The vulnerability of Directors of Children's Services and Adults Services to critical inspection reports is likely to continue; chief executives, by comparison, will be less vulnerable from this source than they were in the 2000–2008 period. Problems relating to whistleblowing and misconduct issues may also reduce (although to a lesser extent); indeed there have been fewer 'cause celebres' of this nature since 2006, which probably reflects the greater understanding on the part of political leaders as to the expectations and sanctions of the new ethical framework. Political change is likely to continue to pose problems for chief executives from time to time although less so than in a period of sharper ideological difference between parties. The 'new' executive arrangements have now been in place for 10 years and the vast majority of authorities appear to have found ways of adjusting the new division of responsibilities involved, with which both chief executives and council leadership can live. The only major stimuli to further change would be a significant increase in elected mayors (as signalled in the Conservative green paper on local government) or if council leaders began to take more advantage of the formal powers bestowed on them by the 2007 Local Government Act (a change for which there is to date very little evidence).

The crucial new element of this context within which leaders and chief executives operate is of course the impact of the recession. The constraining effects of the recession in both financial and policy terms are already becoming apparent. There is clearly a situation developing where there is an increasing likelihood of 'bad news' and 'unwelcome messages' necessarily conveyed by chief executives to political leaders. The recession may also sharpen the differences between the major parties in identifying how best to respond to the social and economic fallout from the recession, as has already been illustrated by the very different approaches adopted in the Conservative controlled London Borough of Barnet (The 'Easy Council') and the Labour Controlled London Borough of Lambeth (The John Lewis model). The likelihood is that the recession will place additional stresses on relationships between leaders and chief executives.

Dealing with a breakdown in relationships

In Chapter 1, the recent Audit Commission report which highlighted the large pay-offs received by 37 chief executives in the 2006–2009 period was discussed, together with some of the reactions to it. It was noted that Bob Neill, in responding to the report, argued that 'there should be no reward for failure, either in the public or private sector', whilst John Denham argued that 'too many chief executives are being dismissed because they have fallen out with council leaders...taxpayers money should not be used to resolve personal differences'.

Both these comments are simplistic responses to a complex problem. Bob Neill's comment about 'reward for failure' make the assumption that chief executives who have received such payments have 'failed'. That is an unwarranted assumption. Some of the chief executive involved could clearly not reasonably be seen as failures. Their 'failure' was that they fell out with their respective leaders, in circumstances where (on the basis of the published evidence) the inappropriate behaviour of the leader was a major factor in the breakdown of the relationship. In some of the cases discussed in Chapter 9 a weak or poor CPA result was a trigger for a political desire for a change of chief executive, but even in this situation, there is an issue of who should bear the responsibility for performance failure of this nature. A less-than-competent chief executive is indeed one possibility, but so is a divisive and obstructive political culture (as in the early 2000s in Hull, Lincolnshire and Walsall) which would and did place major impediments in the way of any chief executive striving to improve performance. The reason why the political leadership may want the chief executive to go may have as much to do with its own failings as the chief executive's if not more so. Certainly a chief executive receiving a substantial pay-off cannot simply be categorised as having failed, as Bob Neill assumes. Was David Henshaw (ex-chief executive of Liverpool) a 'failure'? David Bowles (ex-chief executive of Lincolnshire)? Carol Gilby (the long-suffering chief executive of North East Derbyshire)?

Other findings in the Audit Commission report need to be highlighted to put these headlines and reactions in context. First, the report found that more than a third of council chief executives leaving their jobs between 2007 and 2009 received compensation. By implication almost two-thirds did not do so. The latter are likely to have parted company relatively amicably (typically through retirement or a successful job application elsewhere). Secondly, why is it surprising that one in six of them returned to work in a similar job in a different region? What would one expect a chief executive who has not reached the end of his career and has been obliged to leave a local authority (often in circumstances where they have been more sinned against than sinning) to do? What is perhaps surprising is that it was only one-sixth who followed this course of action. More might have been expected. Thirdly, £9.5m spread amongst 37 authorities over a period of 3years can be regarded as peanuts in the context of the collective overall budgets of the local authorities concerned. Indeed compared with compensation payments made to chief executives who have proved failures in a private sector context, the payments made to local authority chief executives have been relatively modest! Anyone looking for an 'outrageous waste of taxpayers money' would find several other more convincing examples, for example the vast amount of time and energy wasted in the Boundary Committee's recent review of local government structure in Norfolk, Suffolk and Devon. The Secretary of State's view that taxpayers' money should not be used to resolve personal differences is also an oversimplification. It implies that the main issue is typically that leader and chief executive 'don't get on', and (by implication) that they should work harder to find a mutually satisfactory modus operandi. The reality, as we saw in Chapter 9, is that the root of the problem is more often differences of views about the respective roles of leading officers and members, rather than a personal antipathy, although the former may eventually result in the latter. Joint attendance of a 'how to make friends and influence people' course would not, in many cases, resolve the problem.

However, the work of the Audit Commission, and the responses it has generated, do confirm that there is an issue here which needs resolving. What can and should be done when leaders and chief executives fall out is indeed a grey area. If misconduct or maladministration on the part of the latter can be demonstrated following the work of an external assessor, then there are grounds for dismissing a chief executive. If an appraisal system demonstrates major shortcomings in the chief executive's performance (or a Audit Commission report indicates such performance shortcomings on his or her part) then it would be difficult for a chief executive to argue that he or she should continue in post. In any other circumstances, where for whatever reason there has been a breakdown in the relationship (and typically responsibility for the breakdown is a shared one) then the options facing the leader are limited to cajoling, persuading, making life as uncomfortable as possible for a chief executive or if all else fails, negotiating an exit package with him or her. It is hardly surprising that if chief executives feel that the responsibility for the breakdown is largely the fault of a leader, or even that the responsibility is shared, that they should seek such a settlement, rather than resigning prematurely (i.e. before an equivalent or better job had been secured – who wouldn't in such circumstances?). But there must be a better way of dealing with this kind of problem. Appraisal systems, fixed-term contracts, and (more radically) a redefinition of the role of chief executives so that they would become responsible not to the whole council but directly to the executive, who would have the power to hire and fire them are all options worth exploring, which will be considered later in this chapter.

Future developments in the role of chief executives

Although the position of chief executives has survived in the vast majority of authorities, issues have been raised in recent years about whether the job in its current form is vulnerable to redefinition. A series of interlinked questions can be posed which reflect to concerns raised.

First, do local authorities still need chief executives in the light of the introduction of local executive government (mayoral or otherwise)?

Second, can the capacity of a chief executive (or lead officer, however designated) to serve the council as a whole be sustained?

Third, if the answer to either or both of these questions is no, what alternative positions or structures would be more appropriate?

Earlier in this chapter we noted that a small number of councils had decided that they did not need a chief executive position. In 1992 North Tyneside decided to dispense with the post and operated with a system of an executive board of five executive directors (of nominally equal status) who worked with two strong[3] leaders (Brian Flood and Rita Stringfellow). In 2002 the authority changed its mind, in the face of the impending election of a mayor. In 2000, Bristol County Council made chief executive Lucy de Groot redundant (emphasising that 'it was not because of her ability') and operated for 3 years without one, with the role of head of paid service being filled by the director of central services. In 2003, the council changed its mind following its CPA classification as a weak authority and re-created (and subsequently filled) the chief executive position. There have been one or two other examples (e.g. Gravesend) but in each case, the council has over time re-instated the position. The view of David Clark (Director of SOLACE) would appear to be vindicated by these examples.

> Virtually all local authorities which work without a chief executive came back to the idea in the end, as to be excellent you need both strong managerial leadership, and clear political leadership, and you can't combine the two in one person.
> (quoted in *MJ* 26 April 2002)

The four other authorities which have scrapped the post including Thurrock (in 2002), Wyre (in 2002) and Doncaster (in 2004) have replaced the chief executive with an alternative lead officer figure – the 'managing director'. As noted earlier it is not at all clear how a managing director role differs from that of a chief executive.

In 2004 the newly appointed managing director of Doncaster MBC, Susan Law, when questioned about her role as 'managing director' said.

> I don't care what title I have. People ask me what it's like being MD, but I've never thought about it in terms of status. My staff

relate to me as they did my predecessor. I don't see the job as any different from that of a chief executive.

(*MJ* 14 October 2004)

In so far as key differences can be identified, the first appears to be that the managing director is a lower profile role, involving a different balance of power and responsibilities between the managerial and political elites (in favour of the latter). The second is that it is particularly appropriate where there is an elected mayor (as in Doncaster). Susan Law's view is as follows.

> I don't have to manage the politics here. One of the beauties of the mayoral model is that once the council has approved the budget, the mayor can get on and do it...the issue is who has the final executive responsibility – and it's the mayor.
>
> (*MJ* 14 October 2004)

Although it is true that 'managing directors' rather than chief executives have sometimes been advocated in mayoral authorities, the vast majority of such authorities have retained the chief executive position. Susan Law's characterisation of her role evades the issue of serving the whole council. What would have been her role if the council had rejected a mayoral budget, or a scrutiny committee had claimed that it was being refused relevant information from council officers in a review which was legitimately challenging a mayoral decision, through the call-in procedure? Arguably she – or anyone else in that position – would have had to 'manage the politics'.

Challenges to the continuing relevance of the chief executive role have also come from two former Conservative ministers, John Redwood and Michael Heseltine. In 2003 John Redwood[4] argued for the abolition of the role.

> A chief executive in business advising the board on policy and strategy chooses and motivates the team of managers and delivers the results. In local government the ruling group of councillors should set out the policy and strategy, explaining it in the first instance to the electors and then steering it through the officers. This will be easier to do with chief officers responsible for the main

functions and a 'chairman of officers' dealing with the limited number of cross-departmental issues.

(*MJ* 1 May 2003)

The alternative position envisaged here is not seen as a 'managing director', but rather a 'chairman of officers' (with an even lower profile). Redwood adds,

Chief executives are not needed in most government departments, so why should they be required in local government...getting rid of chief executives would force council groups to clarify their objectives more fully and give officers less chance to determine the agenda.

(*MJ* 1 May 2003)

This is an interesting standpoint which clearly reflects a view that officers (in particular chief executives) have too much power, and that something should be done to redress the balance in favour of 'ruling groups' of councillors. The comparison with civil servants breaks down, of course, when it is recognised that their loyalty is to the government, and not to the opposition parties (nor indeed the backbencher members of the party who form the government). Chief executives – or indeed any alternative position – would, under the existing constitutional arrangements, retain a responsibility to serve the council as a whole, not just the executive. If legislation were changed to introduce a civil service model into local government (with separate support for the council as a whole) then the 'chairman of officers' seems an extremely lightweight post compared to that of cabinet secretary. There is also the relevant consideration that at present, there are many executives which would not wish to take the pro-active 'hands-on' kind of leadership role forward by John Redwood.

In 2006 Michael Heseltine expressed a similar view.

Councils do not need both chief executives, who are unaccountable and the highest paid people in most cities, and leaders.... I believe the time has come to combine these two jobs. I believe great cities should elect great leaders and hold them to account...they should be elected by the constituency of the whole city, and not just a constituency which is often unrepresentative of it.

(*MJ* 13 April 2006)

The denial of accountability to chief executives implies a limited and partial view of what constitutes accountability. Lord Heseltine's proposals are clearly linked to an 'elected mayors' sub-text, and indeed if elected mayors were to become the norm, and if the range of real powers available to local authorities were extended well beyond their current limits, there might be a case for taking the proposal seriously. But in the current absence of both conditions, the value of scrapping of chief executives seems inappropriate, in the light of the reality of the way responsibilities are distributed between political and managerial leaders in the vast majority of authorities.

In a world where many of the attitudes to the appropriate roles of leading members and officers continue to be strongly influenced by pre-2000 Act traditions and experiences, the visionary ideas of John Redwood and Lord Heseltine are of intellectual interest, but limited relevance. Of greater relevance is the continuing tension (usually latent rather than manifest) between the responsibility of chief executives to serve the needs both of the cabinet and of the council as a whole. Prior to the 2000 Act, this tension was much less apparent. Chief executives and other directors briefed and serviced all-party committees (including the cabinet-equivalent Policy and Resource Committee), and provided information on request to all members (within generally accepted but sometimes contested opinions as to what the 'right to information' of opposition and backbench members comprised). There were also, of course, meetings with leaders and committee chairs where more sensitive information was shared and options considered in a private setting. But this practice was invariably accepted (at least in principle) by all parties, in that all parties stood to benefit from it when in power.

The feasibility of a unified officer structure

The 2000 Act, by separating out the 'executive' and 'scrutiny' role, raised major issues about the viability of the 'unified officer structure' and, in particular, introduced a much more explicit tension in the chief executive's role. As noted in Chapter 11, it is clear (as would have been predicted) that the dominant role of the chief executive and other chief officers, is to advise, protect and defend the cabinet. In this they are operating in civil service mode, as de facto permanent secretaries. However, in the responsibility to continue to serve the council as a whole, the chief executive and other directors are not like senior civil servants, who are under no obligation to advise support or even provide information to non-members of the executive (except in response to parliamentary questions or select committee inquiries).

This dilemma of 'two hattedness' is most vividly manifested in the way chief executives respond to the demands of the overview and scrutiny function, which, in the light of their responsibilities to the whole council, they might reasonably be expected to support and facilitate, ideally on a parity with their level of support to the executive (although such 'party of esteem' is hardly even approached in most authorities). In parliament, select committees have an independent source of help and advice from civil servants expressly detached from the departments of state. In local authorities there is at best a scrutiny support unit of 2–5 middle-ranking officers embedded with a directorate structure at whose head will be an officer with direct responsibilities (and a direct line) to the cabinet.

In Chapter 11 it was noted that whereas in principle, there is great potential in the executive/scrutiny division for generating role conflict for chief executives, to an extent that would justify a re-assessment of whether the joint responsibilities of the chief executive to these two functions can be sustained, in practice this potential has rarely been realised to any great extent. However, the illogicalities in the current arrangements justify a detailed analysis of the implications for changes in the chief executive's role definition.

Other commentators – in particular the Audit Commission – have recognised the potential and raised similar concerns.

> The need to advise councillors on the executive as well as providing advice to members of the panels may lead to some tensions. Some authorities report that where chief officers are involved in advising cabinet members they are often regarded as biased by overview and scrutiny members.
>
> (Pinder and Dawson 2001)

A key question in new constitutional settlements is whether a unified officer structure can and should survive the widening distinctions between executive and scrutiny roles among members. Certainly legislation requires that the council remains a single employer, but questions remain about the degree of accountability that various officers will owe to the different branches of the political structure.

(Audit Commission 2001)

SOLACE, however, have argued strongly for the retention of the unified officer structure (but then they would, wouldn't they)!

The executive/scrutiny split is producing a number of potentially divisive organisational solutions arrived at to satisfy a rigid interpretation of Government guidance. SOLACE is anxious to promote a whole council approach... without the need for consequent radical structural changes.

(quoted in Fox, Skelcher and Lyons (2002))

The Audit Commission also recognises that the inherent tensions in the 'unified officer structure' are likely to be greater under elected mayors.

Where there is radical change in political structures, more radical consequences for officer structures are likely to be felt. For example, a directly elected executive mayor facing strong political opposition from the council may lead to more radical readjustments in officer arrangements than a council adopting the leader/executive model in a climate of reasonable harmony between the executive and scrutiny roles.

(Audit Commission 2001)

There is a possible future development which may put further pressure on the 'unified officer structure' model. One of the proposals in the Conservative Party's recent Policy Green Paper (Control Shift: Returning Power to Local Communities) is the holding of referenda in England's 12 largest cities as to whether residents wish to have an elected mayor. Currently, apart from Greater London, there are no 'large cities' which have opted for an elected mayor model (apart from Stoke-on-Trent which recently reverted to the leader and cabinet option). If in at least some of these cities the referenda support the introduction of an elected mayor, then two repercussions are likely. First elected mayors are likely to spread to other cities (if Liverpool has one, Manchester will want one, if Leeds then Sheffield). Secondly in cities of this size and tradition of politicisation, pressure will increase to replicate the arrangements which exist in Greater London where there are separate structural elements advising the Mayor and the Assembly respectively.

What would be the alternatives to the status quo (chief executive and unified officer structure) if the tensions identified became more overt? A research report by Fox and Leach (1999) for the Local Government Information Unit addressed this question. After reviewing the research evidence and considering the detailed implications of the new legislation, they concluded that it was important at the very least, that a wider agenda on officer roles and structures should be explored. They noted the mismatch between the radical nature of the changes on the member side and the status quo (or at best incremental changes) perceived as appropriate on the officer side. Three different models of officer structure were identified – the status-quo, a 'limited split' and a 'total split' (see Table 12.2).

In reality, 10 years on from the introduction of local executive government, almost all local authorities have persisted with the unified officer structure. Some (although not all) elected mayors have a mayoral support unit which works exclusively for the mayor (Greater London provides the most elaborate example). A majority of local authorities now have dedicated scrutiny support units but these are not formally separated from the mainstream officer structure. A few authorities have a similar unit (of de facto secondees) who play a similar dedicated support role to the cabinet, under similar circumstances. Some, but not many authorities, have 'political advisors' for each party which can be appointed under the terms of the Local Government Act 1991. However, given the restrictions on their job status, their role is usually a relatively low key one.

In the limited split option, the unified officer structure would be breached in two ways. The chief executive (as head of paid service) would lose control of the cabinet office (appointed directly by the cabinet and answerable to them) and the scrutiny support officer

Table 12.2 Three Models of Officer Structure: Key Features

	Model A Status Quo	Model B Limited Split	Model C Total Split
Responsibilities of Chief Officers	All chief officers serve both executive and assembly functions (including scrutiny)	All chief officers serve both executive and assembly, although work programme dominated by executive agenda.	Most chief officers (including chief executive) are directly responsible to cabinet, both for policy advice and implementation. Assembly has a separate officer support system, with a chief support officer. The 'monitoring officer' and 'financial proprietary' roles are attached to the assembly, as are the regulatory roles and officer structures (and the Standards Committee).
Support for Cabinet, Scrutiny or area Functions	Administrative support to scrutiny and area functions allocated to individual officers as part of their workload. Officers provide reports and advice for cabinet/scrutiny/area functions on request	Cabinet supported by small but powerful 'cabinet office', whose key tasks are research, briefing, progress-chasing, speech-writing and networking. Scrutiny and area functions serviced and supported by parallel dedicated 'office'.	
Appointments of Senior Officers	All appointments made by assembly (or panel thereof)	Cabinet makes appointments to cabinet office; assembly makes senior appointments to scrutiny and area offices, and all other senior officer appointments.	Cabinet appoint chief officers. Assembly appoints chief officers who support their functions
Career Implications	Pattern of career opportunities and paths remains unchanged	Relatively unaffected, although officers may choose to specialise in cabinet/scrutiny/area support roles, or move into and out of such roles from mainstream.	Major implications, e.g. fixed term contracts attached to duration of administration for officers appointed by executive

(appointed directly by full council and answerable to it). In relation to the cabinet office, the chief executive would be faced with an independent group of specialist advisors, a situation with which permanent secretaries have long had to come to terms. The scrutiny office would be likely, in most circumstances, to need an ally or champion within the group of senior mainstream officers, not least to safeguard scrutiny's right to information and advice, which they would need to challenge cabinet proposals or decisions. The council's monitoring officer would be one option (in which case this position could of course not be held by the chief executive). The head of performance review, if such a position existed and was of sufficient status, would be an alternative. In either case the incumbent would need some kind of 'guarantee of independence' from the cabinet (and the chief executive) adding further to the erosion of the 'unified officer' principle. However, the various changes discussed would mean that this principle would survive more or less intact, the changes being marginal rather than fundamental.

Much more fundamental would be the changes involved in the total split. Under this option, the unified officer principle would not survive. The role of head of paid service would disappear. The chief executive – or whatever new title was devised for him or her – would be a political appointment, with an exclusive responsibility to the executive (or 'government') but none to the full council or assembly. Most chief officers (indeed most council officers at all levels) would work (under the chief executive) directly for the cabinet, providing policy advice and implementing its policies and decisions. The assembly would have a separate officer support system – much smaller in size, but with the key regulatory functions, including those of monitoring officer and financial proprietary officer.

There is one anomaly in existing arrangements that would need to be dealt with for the total split option to work. Development (planning) control is often characterised as a regulatory activity, but in fact it is a hybrid. Much of what it does is indeed regulatory, for example ensuring that minor modifications to houses are consistent with detailed planning regulations, and could appropriately be carried out by officers attached to the assembly. However, other types of planning applications are 'strategic' in that they have a major potential impact on the quality of life in the area – for example an out-of-town shopping centre, a city centre redevelopment scheme or a major new housing proposal on a greenfield site. These are the kind of executive decisions which it would be illogical for the cabinet not to make, given its responsibility for developing the planning framework in the context of which such decisions should be made. There would need to be a split of responsibilities between assembly and cabinet (and split of location of professional staff) based on a sensible set of distinctions between strategic and non-strategic applications.

Political appointments

It has been argued that, although a move to a formal division of officers responsibilities between 'serving the executive' and 'serving the assembly' would make political appointments highly likely (and justifiably so), the retention of a unified officer structure (or something approximating to it) does not provide such justification. Council leaders and their colleagues have long made judgements about the ability of candidates to demonstrate a degree of enthusiasm and commitment to the challenge of implementing their party's priorities, and at times have no doubt speculated on candidates' political sympathies. The Widdicombe Committee of Inquiry into Conduct of Local Authority Business identified examples of more overt political appointments – for example, a chair of social services in one London Borough who was appointed Director of Social Services in an adjacent borough, under the same political control. Such possibilities were eliminated by the Local Government Act 1987, drawn up by the Conservative government in response to the Widdicombe Committee's report, which banned those who were politically active (including of course councillors) from holding senior positions in other authorities.

Since the 1980s political appointments of a more overt nature have not been an issue. However, since the introduction in 2000 of local executive government, the arguments for 'political appointments' have been re-ignited.

> One of the problems is that the government is giving out conflicting messages. On the one hand they are saying they want political arrangements that are very political, and on the other they are saying we mustn't have political chief executive appointments.
> (Simmons-Lewis 2002)

In the 2003–2006 period there was a long-running cause celebre concerning what was perceived to have been a 'political appointment', and which generated the most long-drawn-out case in the Standards Board's (recent) history (at the same time resulting in considerable criticism of its approach). In 2002 Helen Bailey was appointed as Chief Executive of the London Borough of Islington following the re-election of a Liberal Democrat administration (with a much larger majority) earlier that year. Ms Bailey at the time the post was advertised was employed by LB Islington as a senior policy consultant.

> After application, consultant Veredus – which ran the recruitment process – did not recommend her for the shortlist, and graded her a D, but councillors reinstated her onto the shortlist. Mr White (QC for the Standards Board) said a Veredus staff member claimed it did not want to be party to a 'stitch – up' or a recruitment process that was pre-determined. Mr Hitchens (Liberal Democrat leader of LB Islington) denied the appointment was pre-determined.
> (*MJ* 13 October 2005)

The original action which set the process in motion was a complaint to the Standards Board by LB Islington's Labour group leader Mary Greagh about the behaviour of Councillor Hitchins (and another Liberal Democrat, Councillor Margot Dunn) in 'failing to declare on appropriate interest in the appointment of Ms Bailey'. The Standards Board subsequently drew the four other members of the borough's Personnel Sub-Committee, (which included Mary Greach) into the inquiry, which they referred to the Adjudication Panel for England in August 2004.

The basis of the case against Councillor Hitchins was that he and Ms Bailey had been friends over a long period of time prior to her appointment (as well as sharing the same political allegiance). However, in January 2006 all the Liberal Democrat councillors concerned were cleared by the Adjudication Panel of allegations that they had breached the local authority's code of conduct in connection with the appointment of Ms Bailey (Mary Greach, the original whistle-blower, had herself been cleared of any wrongdoing in June 2005 by the Standards Board). Ms Bailey continued to operate as Chief

Executive until 2007, when she was appointed to a prestigious central government post.

What this case highlighted (in addition to raising questions about the mode of operation of the Standards Board) were both the opportunities and dangers of the post – 2000 Act ethical framework which now operates. It is now more feasible for opposition councillors to refer members of the executive to the Standards Board, over allegedly 'political appointments' (or indeed a range of other code of conduct breaches) than it used to be. Any leadership elite contemplating an appointment that might be viewed in this light knows the dangers. But in the aftermath of the long-running Islington saga, which took 4 years from allegation to ultimate resolution, any opposition leader contemplating such an action might well also be uneasy about the possible repercussions, (given the way that the whistleblowing opposition leader in Islington had been drawn into the process, and herself accused of breaching the code of conduct, before being exonerated).

The problem of political appointments is unlikely to generate more than the occasional test case (such as the Islington example) under the present constitutions of local authorities. However, if there was a move to a more overt separation of powers, as discussed earlier in this Chapter12 (pp. 180–83), then there would need to be a change of rules to allow political appointments (with appropriate safeguards). Otherwise the mismatch identified by Simmons-Lewis (see Chapter 12, p. 183 above) would become potentially unmanageable.

Job Security and Fixed-Term Contracts

Some of the cases discussed in Chapter 12 – particularly those involving Jim Brooks, David Henshaw and David Bowles – illustrated the vulnerability of chief executives to irrational behaviour on the part of political leaders. In each case it was made clear to the chief executives concerned that they were no longer wanted. Although in two of the cases a substantial financial settlement (or pay-off) was agreed for the chief executives concerned, their experience (and that of several others including the chief executives of NE Derbyshire, Carole Gilby) raises the issue of whether these should be statutory protection for chief executives, and if so, what form it should take.

The current position is that chief executives currently have 'unique extra protection in employment law to reflect their unique status' (SOLACE 2006, p. 36). A 'designated independent person' must be involved in any suspension which has been going on for longer than 2 months. He or she is appointed by agreement, or in default by the Secretary of State (ibid). The role of the 'designated independent person' has sometimes been filled by a former chief executive (Rodney Brooke in Eastbourne), sometimes by a QC (Jim Kerr in NE Derbyshire).

The SOLACE Commission were emphatic that such arrangements should continue.

> The Commission strongly recommends that they should continue to have statutory protection to protect them from dismissal based on perceived political differences that are not based on underperformance or misconduct.
>
> (SOLACE, 2006, p. 36)

They justify this special protection (which even civil servants do not have) as follows.

> It is clearly related to the fact, that unlike civil servants, politicians are directly responsible for the appointment and dismissal of local authority chief executives, and it must also reflect the problem of managing in a political environment and the need for chief executives to be able to blow the whistle.
>
> (ibid, p. 36)

The report goes on to add,

> When confidence does break down between a leader and a chief executive, attempts should be made to resolve the matter amicably. If this is not possible, we recommend that external auditors should take a stance which has the long-term interests of the council and the citizens it serves at its heart and in a way which is consistent with the way similar disputes have been handled in other authorities.
>
> (ibid)

There are two questions evoked by this proposal. First who should the 'external auditors' be? Secondly what happens when there is no case for suspending (or dismissing) the chief executive and it is recommended that it is in the long-term interests of the council (and citizens) that the chief executive remains in position? The problem here is that the political leadership is unlikely to want the chief executive to remain in positions, despite what the external auditor recommends.

Currently there is a single 'external auditor' (or investigator) appointed. Such an investigator would require an in-depth knowledge of the subtle dynamics of leader/chief executive relationships to be in a position to reach a balanced judgement (apart from cases where the issue involved is alleged bullying of staff by the chief executive, as in Eastbourne in 2006, or similar staff management issues). Chief executives (current and former) would be likely to have such understanding but there is a danger of a tendency on their part to see the problem from the perspective of the chief executive concerned. Political leaders would be likely to have the same kind of understanding, but from a (party political) perspective. It has already been demonstrated how different these perspectives can be. QCs, unless their experience has taken them into the world of leader/chief executive relations, are less likely to have the requisite qualities.

A fairer way of dealing with a suspension/intended dismissal would be to set up a small panel comprising a (former) chief executive – nominated by ALACE or SOLACE, a (former) political leader, nominated by the Association of Councillors, and a third party with a reasonable degree of knowledge who is neither a council leader nor a chief executive. Academics specialising in local government would be one option; senior staff from IDeA another. The advantage of such an arrangement is that it would acknowledge that many leader/chief executive disputes are understandable if one recognises the different perspectives involved. What to a chief executive may be 'a leader making unrealistic demands regarding the implementation of his party's manifesto' may to the leader be 'a chief executive digging his or her heels in and putting barriers in the way of our legitimate political agenda'. Hence the dangers of relying solely on a former chief executive (or indeed a former leader) to arbitrate.

What is the best response to the second question – what should be done when a chief executive has been exonerated by the investigation and the recommendation is that he or she remains in position? It could be argued that in these circumstances, and whoever is primarily responsible for the breakdown in the relationship, the continuation of both chief executive and leader in position is unsustainable. The behavioural ingredients for a good relationship are unlikely to be present; nor are they likely to be re-creatable, given the unwelcome nature of the external auditors decision as far as the leader is concerned. Unfortunately, in this kind of situation there is little to be gained by the chief executive remaining in post.

What might prove a better basis for dealing with this kind of situation is the introduction of 'contracts' for chief executives, probably for a 4 yearly term (to correspond with the electoral cycle in many authorities). As the end of the 4-year period either party can seek to extend the contract, but either party has the freedom not to do so. This mechanism would be helpful to chief executives who feel that they have achieved as much as they can in one authority, but hesitate to apply for jobs elsewhere because of the problems this would cause (or be seen to cause) for the chief executive/leader relationship, if the former is unsuccessful in his or her job application(s). It would be an essential innovation if there was a movement to political appointments of chief executives, predicated on a split of functions between executive and assembly (see Chapter 12, pp. 183–185 above).

If the contract included performance specifications and an annual appraisal system (in which the council leadership was a key player) then, if there was a breakdown in the relationship of the type described above, it would be relatively easy to establish whether it reflected a performance failure on the part of the chief executive *or* a changed predisposition on the part of the political leadership (which could reflect a change in party control, or a change in the individual leading the party in control). If there were no performance grounds for dismissing the chief executive, the council would be expected to properly compensate him or her for the premature termination of the contract, which they would have to think very carefully about, in the light of potential media coverage ('chief executive's £300,000 pay-off in cash-strapped Fishport').

The use of fixed-term contracts is in principle more straightforward in authorities in which elections are held every 4 years, rather than three in 4 years (as in metropolitan districts, some unitary authorities and some shire districts). In the former case, if the fixed-term contract is linked to the electoral cycle the incoming party can choose whether or not to offer the incumbent chief executive a new contract. The former choice would be more likely if there were a continuity of political control, but in authorities with a tradition of low-key political partisanship, it is by no means unlikely that the new administration would be happy to continue with the existing chief executive. In the latter case, particularly if one considers politically volatile and partisan councils such as Hull, Walsall, Rochdale and Bristol, the situation would be more complex. Within the first or second year of a chief executive's contract, there could be a different political administration, which may feel that it wants to work with someone it has appointed. In these circumstances, the appraisal system would be a valuable resource. If it demonstrated good performance on the part of the chief executive and a positive evaluation from the (former) leader, then the incoming party would at least be clear that it had to negotiate a severance package, which acknowledged that there was no problem about the chief executive's performance.

Chief Executives and Monitoring Officers

Some of the cases discussed in Chapter 9 suggest that there are advantages in a chief executive not also holding the 'monitoring officer' role. If there is the need for whistleblowing, it is less problematical for a legal officer who is not the chief executive to undertake it, rather than chief executives themselves. In interviews, more than one chief executive told me of the hesitation they had felt in instigating procedures of this kind, knowing the disruptive effect such as action would be likely to have on the relationship with the leader. For chief executives it is very much a 'last resort' option.

However, for another chief officer to be able to play the monitoring officer role effectively, there would need to be a strengthening and clarification of the role. The monitoring officer too would need 'statutory protection' of at least the level currently enjoyed by chief executives. The whistleblowing role is always likely to be politically contentious, but there will be occasions where it is essential that it is carried out without detriment to the officer's position in the authority. Secondly he or she ideally requires a status within the authority that is by no means always provided.

A report for the Standards Board for England carried out by the Universities of Teesside, Warwick and Liverpool in 2004 revealed that monitoring officers were 'struggling to cope'.

> Local government monitoring officers are failing to get on top of the task created by the council/cabinet system. Their duties are sometimes frustrated by lack of seniority, training and support... 'about 25% of monitoring officers are struggling (said Professor Lawton) most, if not all, combine this role with another job, such as head of legal services'... the worst problems come where they were not a part of the senior management team... there were also potential conflicts of interest where they were expected to combine an advisory role with that of investigating complaints of unethical behaviour by their own senior politicians.
> (*MJ* 16 September 2004)

Under a 'division of responsibilities' system (see Chapter 12, pp. 182–183 above), the appointment of the monitoring officer would clearly fall within the remit of the whole council, to whom he or she would be responsible. When the executive needed legal advice, it would have to be provided by a 'legal advisor' working as a member of the cabinet support team. Such an arrangement would avoid the conflict of interests identified in the above quotation, and it would also avoid the subversion by the leader of the monitoring officer's proper role as happened in Lincolnshire CC. It would also provide a further safeguard for monitoring officers, in that if the executive felt that the monitoring officer should be suspended, it would have to persuade the full council, which would usually be very difficult except perhaps in authorities dominated by one particular party.

Can such safeguards be replicated within the existing unified officer structure model? Up to a point they can. First the monitoring officer appointment should be an explicit appointment[5] made by a panel of councillors which (ideally) should not contain members of the executive. If there are other legal responsibilities attached, as is likely, they should relate to advice sought by and provided to the council per se, rather than the executive, who whilst having access to the monitoring officers legal advice if they wished to seek it should also have access to alternative channels of advice, if there is a danger of conflict of interests (legal 'second opinions' are of course common practice). These should also be similar statutory procedures to deal with suspensions to those advocated for chief executives (see Chapter 12, pp. 186–190 above). By strengthening the independence of the role and protecting it from arbitrary political challenge, there would be less need to ensure that monitoring officers were members of the management team, as suggested by the 2004 research team. Indeed there might be real advantages in detaching the monitoring officer from a team that will inevitably look towards the interests of the executive.

Conclusion

The role of local authority chief executive is a demanding and vulnerable (though increasingly well-paid) one. It operates at the interface between the world of politics and the (linked) worlds of professionalism and management. Thus one of the crucial skills of a chief executive is the ability to negotiate with leading members (particularly the council leader) at this interface, understanding the difference between managerial and political agendas, and seeking to respond positively to the latter without undermining the former. It involves judgements of when to give way to political pressure which is likely to result in managerial problems for the chief executive and/or his or her senior colleagues, and when to 'dig ones heels in' and resist such pressure, explaining of course to leaders why it is necessary to take this line. Underpinning such judgements there is usually the idea of a 'bottom line' not in terms of balance sheets but rather reflecting the level below which there is no scope for negotiation and concessions. Nonetheless chief executives sometime decide to depart from the bottom line, taking care (if they are wise) that they make it clear that they are doing so in untypical (and unlikely to be repeated) circumstances.

The value of a 'new institutionalism' perspective in explaining and making sense of the way in which chief executives operate in the political context which is such a crucial element – arguably the most crucial element – of their job has been well demonstrated by the content of the previous chapters. In particular the tensions between leaders and chief executives which have developed around the need to respond to the two external challenges which dominated the agendas of local authorities in the 2000–2008 period – the introduction of executive structures and the impact of the CPA process operated by the Audit Commission (see Chapter 11) – demonstrated the relevance of this perspective. Both externally-imposed government initiatives posed threats to the traditional 'way we do things around here' values and practices of local authorities. Most leading politicians saw these new initiatives as threats to well-embedded traditional practices. The requirement to introduce cabinet government threatened their long-term attachment to the committee system and the dominant role of the party group. The expectations which (it soon became apparent) were associated with the CPA process threatened (amongst other things) the political traditions of 'keeping our options open' (particularly in pre-election years) and, in some cases, a tradition of involvement in micromanagement. Chief executives were only too well aware that cabinet government had to be introduced, subject to specific constitutional requirements, however great the level of political antipathy to the idea. They also knew that to achieve a good or excellent (or even a fair) corporate assessment rating from the Audit Commission their authorities had to be able to demonstrate a range of qualities in their approach to issues such as strategy, performance monitoring, partnership working and overview and scrutiny which might also be inimical to established political practices. Chief executives were thus drawn into negotiations with political leaders where their predisposition to meet the requirements of the 2000 Local Government Act and to increase the chances of a positive CPA evaluation came up against established political institutions which in many cases made the achievement of both objectives more difficult.

Thus in many authorities, the tendency of local political leaders to follow a 'path dependency' course of action, which typically rejected the principles and implications of executive structures and were incompatible with the requirements of the Audit Commission's CPA agenda, had to be reconciled with chief executive's awareness that executive structures had to be introduced and/or that there were unacceptable implications of a weak or poor CPA assessment for the authority (and the chief executive's own credibility).

Several of the insights provided by chief executives when interviewed illustrate these dilemmas.

- The chief executive who identified a 'window of opportunity' to propose executive structures, in a northern authority where the dominant political group was totally opposed to the introduction of such structures.

- The chief executive who negotiated with the council leader to include two priorities in the council's corporate strategy that had not featured in the party's manifesto.
- The chief executive who sought to make the executive's retreat from micromanagement a condition of his employment.
- The chief executive who warned the council leadership that the lack of a corporate strategy with clear priorities would jeopardise the council's chances of a favourable CPA assessment.
- The chief executive who negotiated a compromise budget with the council after the mayor's original proposal had been rejected.
- The chief executive who persuaded her leading members that they had to take seriously the new metropolitan-wide structures and processes (including the multi area agreement), when their predisposition was to do otherwise.

In each example, chief executives were using their negotiating skills to challenge embedded political institutions which were impeding the achievement of 'good performance' (as perceived by influential external agencies such as the Audit Commission or DCLG). As we have seen, the language of new institutionalism, with its emphasis on formal and informal rules, the tenacity of informal elements, the importance of agency and the capabilities of actors and the perception of change as a creative, negotiated and contested process, fits well with the way in which the chief executives interviewed described and interpreted the reality of managing in a political environment, and with the examples (or stories) they used to illustrate this process.

Despite the hazards of the job, most chief executives, most of the time, find a way of operating within a political environment which is at worst satisfactory and at best extremely stimulating and rewarding. Their relationship with their leaders typically covers a similar spectrum. In general they move to another job when they are ready to, not because they are 'forced out' (although some will seek new posts when they feel a growing sense of unease about some aspect of the politics of the authorities in which they work). In interviewing them and listening to their experiences, one derives a mass of accumulated wisdom from which new (or aspiring) chief executives could derive great benefit. In the Postscript which follows, I have attempted to summarise the key elements of that advice.

Postscript

Good Advice for aspiring or new Chief Executives

– Extracted from the insights and experiences of the 30 chief executives interviewed.

1. *Making the application*
   - Find out as much as you can about any authority to which you are thinking of putting in an application. *The Municipal Journal, Local Government Chronicle,* local press searches, Audit Commission CPA reports can all be helpful in this respect. Any personal contacts you have should be exploited. Having digested the recent history of the authority, including its political culture and traditions, decide whether or not to submit an application. If in doubt, submit it. The interview experience (if you get that far) will be beneficial, and you can always withdraw at the interview stage if your doubts become stronger.

2. *The interview*
   - If in the pre-interview discussions, there is the opportunity to learn more from the chief executive about the political and organisational culture, then take it. Watch his or her body language when he is discussing the political leadership. Be prepared to ask searching questions: he or she can always refuse to answer them!
   - At the interview try to draw out as much information as possible about what the politicians expect of you. As you build up

a picture of their priorities, begin to set out your own agenda – the skills you think you possess and the values you hold and your previous experience – in a way which demonstrates relevance to their priorities. But don't promise too much. If you are expected to 'turn the authority round', make a realistic estimate of the time-scale likely to be involved.

3. *Deciding whether or not to take the job*
   - If you are offered the job and are predisposed to take it, check out whether there is all-party support for your appointment. If there is not, use your knowledge of the recent political history of the authority to make an assessment of the risks involved, before deciding whether or not to accept.
   - If you are allowed time to consider whether or not you want to take the job, and you have established a reasonable rapport with the chief executive, then ring him or her for an informal chat to discuss whatever concerns you have. If this does not seem appropriate there may be others you could contact (e.g. the head of personnel) for the same purpose.

4. *The honeymoon period*
   - Unless you have been brought in to deal with a crisis, you can reasonably expect a 'period of grace', when it will be accepted that you need time to learn about the way the authority works. Use it wisely to strengthen your knowledge. Talk to staff at all levels – middle managers and front-line staff as well as directors and heads of service. Talk to 'backbench' councillors (including those from opposition parties) as well as the leadership group. And don't contemplate a structural reorganisation until or unless you are convinced that this is absolutely necessary (which is unlikely to happen during the honeymoon period).
   - At an early stage, seek to initiate a meeting with the leader (ideally in a relaxed, informal setting) to discuss with him or her
     - what is expected of you
     - the leaders preferences in relation to communication/ meetings (e.g. frequency, pattern of phone/e-mail contact, venue of meetings, if and when others should be involved)

- the division of responsibilities between yourself and the leader (including implementation issues, partnership working, dealing with the press etc.).
- any concerns the leader has about the way in which the officer structure has failed to meet the needs of the executive; any evidence of lack of responsiveness, inappropriate behaviour etc.

- If it was not resolved at the job interview, emphasise to the leader that you want to establish links with opposition parties, in a way which will enable you to brief or consult them over issues where it is appropriate to do so. If necessary explain why you think it is important to do so, and resist pressure to do otherwise (this is, or should be, a 'bottom line' issue).
- Use your judgement as to how you can press the leader to establish a clear division of responsibilities. Some leaders will have thought carefully about this issue, and it should be possible to make good progress. Others, however, won't have done so, and may have only a sketchy idea of 'who should do what'. If this is the case, learn what you can, don't push too hard for a clarification, and use the experience of subsequent meetings with the leader to develop a view of his or her 'de facto' sense of the appropriate division of responsibilities.
- After you have had one (or more) meeting(s) with the leader to address this agenda, arrange a meeting with your management team (again ideally in an informal setting). Draw out their views about the political culture of the authority, including any difficulties this poses for them in doing a good professional/managerial job. Then share with them your impressions of the political agenda which emerged from the meeting(s) with the leader and the implications for the way the management team works. Emphasise any changes in officer responsiveness to politicians which you think are necessary, and give them reassurances that you will follow up any concerns they may have about member–officer relations.
- By the end of the honeymoon period (6–9 months into the job) make an assessment of the strengths and weaknesses of your management team colleagues and decide what action you need to take, if any (mentoring, development activities,

coaching etc.). If there are any management team colleagues who you feel are real obstacles to the changes you want to introduce, then develop a strategy to dealing with the problem (including discussions with political leadership and the individual(s) concerned).
- Use the honeymoon period to develop an in-depth understanding of the political dynamics of the party (or parties) forming the executive and the opposition. Is the leader a 'strong leader' – in the sense of having an ability to persuade his or her colleagues of something he or she has agreed with you (at least most of the time). Who are the leader's key allies within the executive? Is the leader's position at all vulnerable (perhaps as a result of schisms within the party group) or does he or she have enough support to make a change of leader highly unlikely. What are relations like between the leader and the leader(s) of the opposition. If the leader is a weak leader, who are the individuals who are as influential (or more so) – the deputy leader, the chief whip, the portfolio holder for resources? This understanding will help you to deal with the crises which will inevitably occur from time to time.
- At an appropriate time, when you have familiarised yourself with the political culture of the authority, decide what your 'bottom line' is in relation to dealings with the leader: where you would be prepared to compromise, and where your integrity would not permit you to do so.

5. *Managing the Relationship with the Leader*
   - Develop a capacity to 'read the leader'; to develop an understanding of his or her body language, attention span, preferred modes of communication and evidence of impending tension or temper – loss. Recognise that you will have to adjust your behaviour to that of the leader; if his or her attention span is limited, you will have to work within that constraint (although it is OK to have a bottom line in relation to behavioural issues, e.g. no personal criticism of the chief executive (or other officers) in public). Understand too the leaders' political ambitions. Is he or she working towards a parliamentary candidature? Or a senior role in the LGA? Or is the current leadership position the limit of their ambitions?

- If it has not been possible to discuss and establish a division of responsibilities at an earlier stage, look out for specific requests or comments from the leader which raise issues about the division of responsibilities and use opportunities to seek a clarification – for example, if a leader wants to chair a officer working group on 'cleaning up the city', draw out the implications for the involvement of members in operational detail and seek to agree a workable arrangement.
- Start from the premise that it is up to you (all other things being equal) to find a way to enable the leader to achieve what he or she wishes to achieve, although this may mean finding a way of doing something other than the initial preference of the leader. However, if it is clear that an initiative favoured by the leader is not feasible – for political, legal or administrative reasons – make it clear that this is the case (and why it is).
- Seek opportunities to support the leader in his meetings with the public, the media or other agencies (e.g. partnership working). There is often a case not just for a briefing on the substantive issues concerned, but also on the likely stances taken by other actors and agencies, and the best way of responding to them (e.g. 'the Chief Constable is likely to argue X, in which case the best response would be Y'...).
- Don't take the relationship for granted even when it is working well. Watch out for danger signs of staleness and predictability. Try to identify ways of stimulating the relationship, perhaps by identifying new opportunities for the leader to take forward his or her agenda (e.g. by seeking a lead role on a conurbation-wide MAA (multi-area agreement) initiative).
- Ensure that you follow the 'no surprises' principle, especially when 'bad news' rather than 'good news' is involved. In particular make sure that the leader (or other members of the executive) never learn of issues which will be concern to them through the media, or from other sources. You need to be in there first to sustain your credibility.
- The only exception to the general rule of trying to find a way of delivering what a leader wants (assuming it is legal and financial and administratively viable) is if you are convinced what he or she is proposing will be detrimental to the long-term well-being of the area. Use arguments of this nature sparingly,

and only when you can produce evidence to support your view.
- Similarly, if you are clear that there is an opportunity that would benefit the area that should (in your view) be taken, but which the leader is opposed to (or doubtful about) then by all means seek to persuade him or her, again citing evidence to support your view. But don't push it too far; recognise the point when you are clearly not persuading the leader and he or she is becoming irritated and at that stage, drop the subject.
- If you experience a problem with the leader's behaviour or verbal contribution in a public arena – either directed at you or a valued partner – seek to raise the issue as soon as possible after the event (but not, unless the circumstances are exceptional, at the event). Seek to find out why the leader acted as he did (or said what he did) and explain why you found it problematic. Similarly, take seriously any issue of this nature which the leader raises about your behaviour or public utterances, and seek to come to an understanding about it as soon as feasible.

6. *Coping with Political Change*

- Anticipate possible changes of power either of leadership within the dominant party or a change of control at a forthcoming election. Think through what your tactics would be if either of these changes took place, and whether it would be appropriate to make contact with potential new leaders (e.g. seeking a meeting with an opposition leader prior to an election, to discuss the implications of his or her agenda 'if elected').
- Maintain the linkages with all party groups that you (ideally) established soon after your appointment, and offer briefings (or advice as to the feasibility of manifesto commitments) prior to elections, so long as you are confident that this will not undermine your relationship with the existing leader.
- If it is possible that your authority will be 'no overall control' after an approaching election, think through what your tactics will be if that outcome occurs. Make clear your availability for one-to-one discussions with all party leaders the day after the election, and see who shows up.

- If asked for advice about possible coalitions, consider carefully whether you want to act as 'honest broker', intermediary, or to leave negotiations wholly to the politicians. There is no 'right answer'. Much will depend on the pattern of relationships you have formed with party leaders and what role would be acceptable to all of them.
- If negotiations have reached a hiatus, emphasise to all party leaders that a positive outcome must be reached. The council must have an executive. At this stage you may wish to consider changing your role, perhaps from 'facilitator' to 'honest broker'.
- If there is a change of power, and you sense that the new leader doesn't trust you, tackle the issue openly, seek to reassure him or her that you will be as assiduous in implementing the priorities of the new administration as you were with its predecessor, and seek an early opportunity to demonstrate that you can implement one or more of the new administration's priorities.
- If you experience rudeness, in public, from a new leader, keep your cool, don't (over) react, and look for early opportunities to develop a rapport. If the rudeness persists, however, raise it as a 'bottom line' issue with the leader, explaining (in the nicest possible way) why such behaviour is unacceptable.

7. *Safeguarding your position/deciding when to move on*

- Seek to initiate (if one does not already exist) an annual appraisal system of your own performance to which the leader is a major contributor. This will prove a useful reference point if there is a major fall out between the two of you. If your appraisal indicates good performance then if there is pressure for you to go, poor performance cannot be used as an excuse.
- If you are relatively new to the job (or even if you aren't) seek to identify a more experienced chief executive as a mentor; someone you can discuss any problems you have with the leader, or indeed any uncertainties which you have as a chief executive as to how to deal with a situation.
- If serious problems develop in your relationship with the leader, seek out colleagues in other authorities who have experienced similar difficulties and use them as reference points,

comparing experiences and discussing possible ways of resolving your problems.
- If such problems persist, and you are finding it difficult to resolve them directly with the leader then (assuming he or she is agreeable) seek to identify a 'third party' conciliator, with whom you can both discuss your problems, and strive to resolve them. Only if this fails do you need to start thinking about seeking jobs elsewhere.
- If the leader clearly wants you to go, and you are clear that the relationship cannot be repaired, then you probably have to accept that one of you needs to go. If there is little or no prospect of the leader being deposed (either within his or her party group or at an election) then make it clear that you (assuming positive appraisal outcomes) will expect a proper level of compensation.

Notes

Preface

1. Local Political Leadership; Steve Leach and David Wilson, Policy Press 2000.
2. Local Political Leadership in England and Wales, Steve Leach, Jean Hartley, Vivien Lowndes, James Downe and David Wilson, Joseph Rowntree Foundation 2005.
3. Plus I had a large amount of interview-based material for political leaders from previous research, including the 2003–2004 Joseph Rowntree Foundation project.

1 Introduction: Understanding the Challenges Facing Chief Executives

1. See Leach and Wilson (2000, p. 67) for details of sources.
2. As opposed to the service assessments, both the corporate and service assessments contribute to an authority's overall CPA score (see Chapter 9).
3. Although there are increasing difficulties for them in doing so since the introduction of local executive government since 2000 (see Chapter 12).

2 Taking the Job and Getting Started

1. All the material in italics is drawn from the 16 interviews carried out in 2008–2009.

3 The Chief Executive as 'Head of Paid Service'

1. If the chief executive is also the monitoring officer, there is also a major potential tension between this whistle blowing role and the need to develop a productive relationship with leading members.
2. It is rare nowadays for members to be involved in appointments below the top tier of officers (sometimes extended to deputies, or heads of service in a directorate structure). Most chief executives would be strongly resistant to a member involvement in appointments below this level.

5 Dealing with Political Change

1. In some cases of course, the change is from majority control to no overall control. The role which chief executives play in dealing with an NOC situation is discussed in Chapter 7. In this chapter we focus on the development of the relationship once a new council leader has been elected.

8 Testing the Relationship

1. Examples from the 2005 JRF research are also included where appropriate.
2. In some cases examples fit into more than one category. The dominant category is the one recorded.
3. See Chapter 5 for further examples of the problems which can be caused by deposed or reinstated leaders.

9 Moving On: By Choice or Otherwise

1. The material used in this chapter is taken directly from pages of *Local Government Chronicle* or the *Municipal Journal*. I have no 'insider knowledge' of these cases; my interpretation rests on what has been reported. The problems reviewed include those which were faced by chief executives in LBs of Islington, Hillingdon, Harrow and Bromley, Lincs CC, the unitary authorities of Thurrock, Swindon, Hull, Birmingham and Liverpool and the shire districts of Erewash, Cheltenham, North East Derbyshire, Eastbourne and Waverley.
2. It is important to note that the chief executive did not initiate the legal proceedings which led to the leader's conviction.
3. In fact he was appointed to a high-profile government post in 2007.

10 The Impact of Inspection and the Performance Culture

1. The CPA has been replaced by Comprehensive Area Assessments (CAAs), but at the time of my interviews (2008–2009) these were at a relatively early stage of development, and its impact on leader/chief executive relationships was speculative rather than evidence-based.
2. In all subsequent quotes from CPA reports for individual authorities, the source is the Audit Commission.

11 The Impact of the Move to Executive Government

1. The sixth had been a council leader, but not within the previous 8 years.

12 Where Next for Chief Executives

1. In the case of JRF interviews, this was established through interviews with the leaders concerned; in the more recent (2008–2009) interviews the perception of the chief executive was accepted.
2. Eastbourne and Erewash provide (at least partial) exceptions to this conclusion.

3. Strong in the sense of having a clear vision for the area, and a hands on approach to its achievement.
4. In a policy paper for the think tank 'Politeia'.
5. Rather than the role subsequently allocated to someone appointed to a different position (e.g. Borough Secretary, Borough Solicitor, Head of Legal Services).

Bibliography

Audit Commission (2001) *To Whom Much Is Given*. Abingdon: Audit Commission.
Copus C (2006) *Leading the Localities Executive Mayors in English Local Government*. Manchester: Manchester University Press.
Elcock H (2001) *Political Leadership*. Cheltenham: Edward Elgar.
Exworthy M (2000) *Working Relations between Chairs and Chief Executives in Registered Social Landlords*. London: Housing Corporation.
Fox P (1998) *Strengthening Local Democracy: Dealing with Problems of Member Conduct*. London: SOLACE Enterprises.
Fox P and Leach S (1999) *Officers and Members in the New Democratic Structures*. London: LGIU (Local Government Information Unit).
Fox P, Skelcher C and Lyons M (2002) *Continuity or Change? Officers and the New Constitutions*. London: DTLR.
Gains F (2004) 'The Local Bureaucrat: A Block to Reform or a Key to Unlocking Change' in Stoker G and Wilson D (2004).
Gains F, Greasley S, John P and Stoker G (2009), 'The Impact of Political Leadership on Organisational Performance: Evidence from English Local Government', *Local Government Studies* 35 (1) pp. 75–94.
Game C (1979) 'Review Essay: On Political Leadership' *Policy and Politics* 7 (4) pp. 395–408.
Greer A and Hoggett P (1997) 'Patterns of Governance in Local Spending Bodies' *International Journal of Public Sector Management* 10 (3) pp. 214–227.
Judge D, Stoker G and Wolman H (1995) *Theories of Urban Politics*. London: Sage Publications.
Gyford J, Leach S and Game C (1989) *The Changing Politics of Local Government*. London: Unwin Hyman.
Kotter J and Lawrence P (1974) *Mayors in Action: Five Approaches to Urban Governance*. New York: John Wiley.
Leach S (2006) *The Changing Role of Local Politics in Britain*. Bristol: Policy Press.
Leach S (2009) *Party Politics and Scrutiny in Local Government: Clearing the Hurdles*. London: Centre for Public Scrutiny.
Leach S (2010) 'The Audit Commission's View of Politics: A Critical Evaluation of the CPA Process' *Local Government Studies* 36 (3) pp. 445–462.
Leach S and Lowndes V (2007) 'Of Roles and Rules: Analysing the Changing Relationship between Political Leaders and Chief Executives in Local Government' *Public Policy and Administration* 22 (2) pp. 183–200.
Leach S and Stewart J (1992) *The Politics of Hung Authorities*. London: Macmillan.

Leach S, Hartley J, Lowndes V, Wilson D and Downes J (2005) *Political Leadership in England and Wales*. New York: Joseph Rowntree Foundation.

Leach S, Pratchett L and Wingfield M (1997) *All You Need is Trust? The Changing Relationship between Officers and Members*. London: Local Government Management Board.

Leach S and Wilson D (2000) *Local Political Leadership*. Bristol: Policy Press.

Lowndes V (2004) 'Reformers or Recidivists: Has Local Government Really Changed?' in Stoker G and Wilson D (eds) (2004) pp. 230–246.

Lowndes V and Leach S (2004) 'Understanding Political Leadership: Constitutions, Contexts and Capabilities' *Local Government Studies* 30 (4) pp. 557–575.

Marsh D and Stoker G (2002) *Theories and Methods in Political Science*. London: Palgrave.

National Federation of Housing Associations (1995) *Competence and Accountability*. London: NHFA.

Pinder K and Dawson H (2001) *Under New Management*. London: IDeA (unpublished).

Ranson S and Stewart J (1994) *Management for the Public Domain*. London: Macmillan.

Roberts M and Leach S (2010) 'Local Political Context of the Recession' in J Richardson (ed) *From Recession to Renewal*. Bristol: Policy Press (forthcoming).

Selznick P (1957) *Leadership in Administration*. New York: Harper and Row.

Simmons-Lewis S (2002) 'Skills Shortage sees Salaries soar Sky-high' *Local Government Chronicle* 11 January 2002.

SOLACE (2006) *Managing in a Political Environment*. London: SOLACE.

Stewart J (2000) *The Nature of the British Local Government*. Basingstoke: Macmillan.

Stewart R (1989) *Leading in the NHS: A Practical Guide*. Basingstoke: Macmillan.

Stoker G and Wilson D (2004) *Local Government Towards the 21st Century*. Basingstoke: Palgrave/Macmillan.

Stone C (1995) 'Political Leadership in urban politics' in D Judge et al. (1995).

Widdicombe D (Chair) (1986) *Report of the Committee of Enquiry into the Conduct of Local Authority Business*.

Index

Adjudication Panel for England, 184
Association of Councillors, 187
Association of Local Authority Chief Executive (ALACE), 187
Audit Commission, xi, xiv, 1, 13, 15, 28, 115, 121–2, 130–3, 134, 136–7, 142–3, 146, 149, 156, 171, 172–3, 178, 191–3

Bailey, Helen, 184–5
Barnet, London Borough of, 171
Barnsley MBC, 28
Best Value, 130, 148
Birmingham City Council, 119
Blackburn and Darwen Council, 155
Blunkett, David, vii
Boundary Committee, 172
Bowden, Mike, 115
Bowles, David, 2, 117–18, 122, 124, 172, 185
Boynton, Sir John, vii
Bradley, Wareen, 125, 126
Bristol City Council, 29, 169, 174
Bromley, London Borough of, 119
Brooke, Rodney, 186
Brooks, Jim, 120–1, 124, 170, 185
budget setting, 79, 140–1, 161, 175
Bundred, Steve, 116

cabinet government (local), 130–1, 150–63
Camden, London Borough of, 4
central government comparisons (role of chief executive), 20–1
Centre for Public Scrutiny (CfPA), 153
Cheltenham BC, 2, 118–19, 124, 126, 169

Chief executives
briefing the opposition, 49–50, 62–3, 81–2
changing the culture, 39–40
and the CPA system, 131–2, 134–6
as custodians of the interests of the area, 78–82, 103–4
dealing with changes in political control, 62–8, 199–200
future developments, 173–91
head of paid service role, 38–47
job applications and interviews, 26–31, 194–5
managing in hung authorities, 76–8, 198–9
period of grace, 31–7, 195–7
pressures of the job, 1–4, 164–6
relationship with council leaders, viii, 3–4, 9, 31–7, 48–61, 62–70, 85–96, 97–108, 197–201; causes of breakdown in relationship, 166–72; dimension of good relationships, 22–5, 83–96, importance of negotiation, 87–90, problematic circumstances, 28–9, 44–7, 68–70, 90–2, 97–108, 111–28, 200–1
relationship with management team, 38, 40–4, 99–101
role in manifesto drafting, 75–6
significance of leader/group relations, 50–3
'whistleblower' role, 74–5, 116–19, 167, 170, 189–91
Children's Trusts, 105–6
Clark, David, 174

207

Cockell, Merrick, 116
codes of conduct, 116
Comprehensive Area Assessments (CAA), 170
Comprehensive Performance Assessments (CPA), ix, 11, 12, 15, 22, 23, 27, 28, 32, 35, 42, 50, 55, 60, 67, 101, 102, 104–8, 110, 112, 113–16, 121, 123, 127, 130–49, 153–5, 166–8, 170, 174, 191–3
Coventry MBC, 4
Crime and Disorder Partnerships, 16, 146–7
Critical incidents, 97–9
  being the bearer of bad news, 97–108
  dealing with difficult political circumstances, 107–8
  dealing with 'inappropriate behaviour', 106–7
  establishing credibility by decisive action, 99–101
  management issues, 101–4
  persuading a reluctant leader, 104–6
Croft, Ian, 118, 122, 126

Dear, Eric, 4
de Groot, Lucy, 174
De Montfort University, vii
Denham, John, 1, 171
Department of Communities and Local Government (DCLG), 1, 90, 101, 193
development planning, 182–3
Devon County Council, 172
directors of children's services, 113, 170
directors of social services, vii, 113, 183
district audit, 117, 121
Doherty, Paul, 114
Doncaster MBC, 161, 174
Dunn, Margaret, 184

Ealing LBC, 3
Eastbourne BC, 186, 187
eco towns, 80, 90
elected mayors, 17, 156–62, 177
  gradualists, 160–1
  insiders, 159–60
  visionaries, 158–9
Erewash DC, 169

Filkin, Geoff, 4
Finnegan, Matt, 125
fixed term contracts, 110, 185–9
Flood, Brian, 174
Foreign Office, 21
Fox, Pam, 17, 28, 68–9, 180
Further Education Colleges, 18

Gains, Francesca, 17
Game, Chris, 13
Gilby, Carole, 172, 185
Grant, Bernie, vii
Gravesend DC, 174
Greach, Mary, 184
Greater London Authority (GLA), 21, 167, 179–80

Halsall, Phil, 125
Halton, Derek, vii
Harrow LBC, 127
health authorities, 19
Henshaw, Sir David, 124–6, 172, 185
Heseltine, Lord, 175–7
Hillingdon LBC, 115, 124, 169
Hitchens Councillor, 184
Homer, Lin, 119–20
hospital trusts, 18
housing action areas, xi
housing associations, 18, 19
hung authorities, 76–8, 198–9

IDeA, 187
Inglis, Colin, 121, 124
Institute of Local Government Studies, vii
institutional theory, 4–9, 191–3
Islington BC, 2, 4, 169, 183–5

Joseph Rowntree Foundation, vii

Kensington and Chelsea LBC, 116
Kerr, Jim, 186
Kingston-on-Thames LBC, 2
Kingston-upon-Hull City Council (sometimes referred to as Hull City Council), 28, 29, 113, 120, 169, 170, 171
Kotter, J.P., 13

Laird, Christine, 118–19
Lambeth, London Borough of, 171
Lancashire County Council, 28
Law, Susan, 161, 174
Lawrence, P.R., 13
Leach, Steve, xi, 4, 7, 9, 10, 12, 13, 137, 180
leadership style, 29
Leadership tasks, 11–17
  ensuring good performance and the delivery of priorities, 13, 16
  ensuring a stable decision-making environment, 13–15, 71–6
  providing a clear strategic direction, 13, 15
  using external networks to further priorities, 13, 15, 16
leadership theory, xi, xii
Lear, Tony, 128
Leatham, Duncan, 116
Leicester Business School, xi
Lincolnshire County Council, 2, 113, 117–19, 121–2, 126–7, 169, 171, 190
Liverpool City Council, 2, 124–5
Livingstone, Ken, vii
local executive government, viii, 150–63
Local Government Acts
  1987, 183
  1991, 180

2000, vii, 5, 9, 150, 156, 162, 167, 177, 192
2007, vii, 130, 151, 156, 162–3, 170
Local Government Association (LGA), 55
Local Government Chronicle (LGC), 2, 109, 167
Local Government Information Unit, 180
Local Government Management Board, vii
Local Strategic Partnerships (LSPs), 16, 140, 146–7
Lowndes, Vivien, 5, 9, 137

managing director role, 169–70, 174–5
Manchester City Council, vii
Markham, Joyce, 127
McKinley, Andrew, 118–19
monitoring officers, 189–91
Municipal Journal (MJ), 2, 109, 167

Neill, Bob, 1, 171
Norfolk County Council, 172
North East Derbyshire DC, 124, 172, 185
North East Lincolnshire Council, 169
North Shropshire DC, 148
North Tyneside MBC, 28, 113, 142, 169, 174

OFSTED, 41, 113, 114, 130–1
overview and scrutiny function, 153–5, 177–8

partnership working, 146–7
performance management, 17, 141–2
Pointer, Christine, 117
Policy and Resources Committees, 151, 177
policy implementation, 142–6
political advisors, 21, 46, 167

political appointments, 3–5, 18
political leadership, 83–5
political/managerial differences of perspective, vii, x, 9–11, 47, 90–1
Poole BC, 120
Pratchett, L., 10
Primary Care Trusts (PCTs), 18, 170
private sector comparisons (chief executives), 17–18
protocols (in member/officer relations), 47
public and customer involvement, 147–8
public sector comparisons (chief executive), 18–20
Puddifoot, Ray, 116

Ranson, Stuart, 18
Reading BC, 4
Redwood, John, 175–6
Roberts, Mark, 7
Roxburgh, Ian, 4
Royal Town Planning Institute, 28

Selznick, P., 12
Slyfield, Chris, 117
Social Services Inspectorate, 130
Society of Local Authority Chief Executive (SOLACE), 18, 20, 28, 61, 83, 84, 88, 114, 115, 129, 134, 166–7, 174, 178, 186–7
Speechley, Jim, 117–18, 121–2, 124, 126–7
Standards Board, 116, 117, 119–20, 125, 167, 184–5, 190
Stewart, John, 5, 18

Stoke-on-Trent City Council, 17, 28, 29, 113
Stone, Clarence, 12
Stone, Rodney, 114
Storey, Mike, 124–6
strategic priorities, 137–41
Stringer, Graham, vii
Stringfellow, Rita, 174
Suffolk County Council, 172
Swindon BC, 114

Telford and Wrekin Council, 3
Thurrock Council, 169, 174
trust (in leader) chief executive relationships, 85–7
Tunbridge Wells DC, 114, 169

unified offices structure, 150, 177–83
alternatives to, 180–3

Veredus, 184

Walsall MBC, 28, 171
Wandsworth LBC, 3
Warwickshire CC, 28
Waverley BC, 117, 119, 169
Westminster LBC, 155
Widdicombe Committee (1985), vii, viii, 183
Wigan MBC, 28
Wilson, David, viii, xi, 12, 13
Wingfield, Melvin, 10
Worcestershire CC, 142, 148
Wyre DC, 174

Yes Minister, 20
Yes Prime Minister, 21